"We wore what we'd got."

Women's Clothes in World War II

Compiled by Maggie Wood

WARWICKSHIRE BOOKS

First published in Great Britain in 1989 by Warwickshire Books

Copyright © 1989 Warwickshire County Council

ISBN: 1–871942–01–2

British Library Cataloguing-in-publication Data

Wood, Maggie
    We wore what we'd got: women's clothes in World War II.
    1. English Fashion, History
    I. Title
    391'.00.942

Typesetting and Artwork by P&M Typesetting Ltd, Exeter
Printed and bound in Great Britain by Penwell Print Ltd

WARWICKSHIRE BOOKS

Official Publisher to Warwickshire County Council

An imprint of Wheaton Publishers Ltd
A member of Maxwell Pergamon Publishing Corporation plc

Wheaton Publishers Ltd
Hennock Road, Exeter, Devon EX2 8RP
Tel: 0392 74121: Telex 42794 (WHEATN G)

SALES
Direct sales enquiries to Warwickshire Books at the address above

Contents

Acknowledgements

Many people have helped in the preparation of this book.

I would like to thank the following women, who, with patience and good humour, have generously provided much of the material used here:

Dorothea Abbott, Lynne Allnatt, Lindsay Barber, Joan Barnsley, Doris Bateman, Enid Broadhurst, Beryl Buckler, Betty Clayton, S. Coldicott, Pamela Crouch, Pauline Currie, Ellen Davis, Ena Dipper, Dot Eccleston, Frances Fish and Leamington Spa Afternoon Townswomen's Guild, Lorna Fothergill, Una Hancock, Joyce Hawkins, Margaret Hooper, Elsie Kersley, Ena Lake, Ethel Loveridge, Anne Milne, Jocelyn Morris, Jean Nealon, Mary Payne, Doris Peat, Joan Pring, Elspeth Redhead, Grace Robbins, Dorothy Robotham, Alice Sanderson, Joan Saunders, Pat Slessenger, Elsie Somerfield, Kate Stephens, Lady Stephens, Peggy Stone, Daphne Tuffin, E. Wager, Edith West, Irene Williams.

Thanks also to

Mrs Burgess of Atherstone
Ann Cooper of Automotive Products, Leamington Spa
Donald Kennedy of G.E.C. – Alsthom Large Machines Ltd, Rugby

and last, but certainly not least,

Eileen Measey and my colleagues at Warwickshire Museum.

Photographs

Extracts from the book *Librarian in the Land Army* by Dorothea Abbott are quoted by kind permission of the author.

Introduction

In 1989, museums throughout Britain commemorated the fiftieth anniversary of the outbreak of the Second World War by organizing displays and exhibitions depicting aspects of life in wartime.

Warwickshire Museum marked the event by mounting a costume exhibition looking specifically at the effect of war on women's dress in the 1940s. Much of the material used in this book was collected during the research for that exhibition. Through the local press, and organizations such as Women's Institutes and Townswomen's Guilds, the museum made contact with local women who were prepared to share their experiences of wartime dress. Some supplied photographs and written accounts, while others were interviewed and recorded on tape. The aim, in collecting and using this material, was not to provide a general history of women's dress in the Forties but to illustrate how certain individuals coped with clothing in difficult times.

The ten years between 1939 and 1949 form an extraordinary decade in the history of women's clothing. The British Government imposed far-reaching restrictions on manufacturers and consumers alike, so that what was bought, how it was made and what it cost all became subject to official control. The mass mobilization of women for war work despatched large numbers to new and unfamiliar jobs where clothing was prescribed. Shortages of previously commonplace goods and materials meant that women had to adapt both their wardrobes and their attitudes to suit the changing times.

In terms of 'fashion', these years are often viewed as drab and dreary. Images spring to mind of women – usually in a queue – dressed in severely tailored coats, with heads bound in turbans. The impression is always one of a nation of women in a kind of civilian uniform, all looking very much the same.

Yet one of the interesting things to emerge from this collection of written and recorded material is that, in spite of restrictions and rationing, some women managed to bring a touch of individuality to their appearance. With patience and imagination they created clothes, shoes and accessories from the most unlikely of materials, and 'customized' plain Utility dresses with embroidery, paint and home-made trimmings. Such garments were not 'high fashion', and not always very elegant, but they ensured that beneath the austerely functional coats and jackets some women were uniquely clad.

"... there weren't many slacks worn before the war — it wasn't the done thing."

1 Clothing by Order

During the Second World War, fashion, like other aspects of life in Britain, became subject to government control. A shortage of labour and materials for the production of civilian clothing led to state restrictions being imposed on both the makers and consumers of clothes. How women dressed was no longer determined by taste and income alone, but by official decree.

Restrictions on dress crept up on the civilian population gradually, from an initial shortage of luxury items like silk stockings early in the war, to the controls placed on manufacturers in 1942 which determined the look of a garment even down to the number of buttons and width of seams. Women's clothes, and their attitudes towards them, underwent considerable change within a very short time.

The first far-reaching measure of control was Clothes Rationing. This came into force from 1st June 1941 and lasted until 1949. Each adult was given sixty-six coupons annually, although this number was later reduced. Coupons had to be surrendered whenever any purchase of clothing, footwear or fabric was made: in 1941 a woman's suit 'cost' eighteen coupons and a pair of shoes five. Magazines carried articles advising on the planning of wardrobes under the new restrictions and drew up tables to show how coupons could best be allocated.

Although everyone was subject to rationing, some women were harder hit than others because they had fewer pre-war clothes. For those on low incomes, or new to work at the outbreak of war, there had been little opportunity to acquire a wide and varied wardrobe.

"I can't say I had a wonderful wardrobe before the war because I hadn't had any money. In my apprenticeship (as a hairdresser) I had 2/6d. the first year and 5/- the second."

"When I started work wages were low. I believe I earned 12/6d. to start with in a shop: 9 a.m. – 7 p.m. Early closing 9 a.m. – 1 p.m. Friday till 8 p.m. Saturday 9 p.m. I received 2/6d. pocket money. Just before my 18th birthday when I went into the Land Army I still hadn't earned much, or been able to get any clothes by me."

Women who already had a good selection of clothes were, in some ways, better placed to deal with the stringencies imposed by rationing.

"My sister ... being four years older, had had the chance to buy clothes before rationing, so had already got a few clothes."

"I'd been in the gown trade virtually all my life up till then and I'd got quite a lot of clothes, so I can't remember ever trying or needing to buy clothes in the war."

Women, whether taking advice from magazines or using their own common sense, managed their coupons according to their individual requirements. Many endeavoured to make do with pre-war garments, while using coupons for essentials.

"We wore what we'd got — from before the war starting. You couldn't buy much. For me, the things you had to replace were stockings and underclothes."

"I think my biggest thing was shoes … thinking about it now, that's where quite a lot of my coupons went."

"Overcoats always … stockings and all underwear, pyjamas … I had one coat for three years — this particular one that I had was a beaver lamb — artificial — I remember seeing it in the window and thinking, 'Oh! I like that'."

Sometimes coupons would be carefully saved in order to have "a little splash" from time to time:

"It was a camel coat with a brown collar and I bought it at C & A when I went home to Cheshire on leave once — because I'd got the coupons together — and you had a little splash then. Just a coat and a dress — I couldn't afford anything else. I didn't have the coupons, you see."

Although the official allocation of coupons numbered sixty-six, there were ways and means of acquiring more. Within families, elderly relatives would gladly give up their own coupons to a young niece or grand-daughter:

"You had a lot of friends who would help you with coupons: three elderly ladies that were friends of my grandmother — they would help."

There was also a roaring trade in unused coupons, referred to in letters and interviews as 'fiddling':

"There was a lot of fiddling. You used to buy coupons and not feel at all guilty … there was always someone who didn't use their coupon ration that would sell them to you."

"I know there was a lot of fiddling went on — people did acquire coupons from other sources."

Another way of overcoming shortages imposed by rationing was to borrow and swap garments with friends and relatives of similar size:

"We helped each other, borrowed for special occasions, raided our mother's and grandmother's clothes cupboards."

"… being a family of four girls we used to interchange a lot with clothes because at that time we were all the same sort of figure … you'd be amazed, you know, what went from one down to the other."

"There was quite a bit of borrowing of clothes. I remember wearing my mother's coat and hat to a wedding in 1945."

As it became more difficult to buy new clothes, many women were less casual about disposing of old ones. Stores and private dressmakers did good business in the remodelling and repairing of garments, including corsets.

Although few women remember jumble sales — "I don't remember a jumble sale because you didn't give your things away — you wore them out" — there was a trade in second-hand clothing. One woman, who lived in the north of England, recalls that wealthier women advertised surplus items for sale in the *Manchester Evening News* and these could be purchased without coupons. Women who had not previously worn second-hand clothes turned to advertisements in the glossy magazines for coupon-free bargains:

" 'The New Poor' — a Dress Agency run by gentlewomen in the interests of gentlewomen."

The dyeing of clothes was another flourishing area for professional renovators, or it could be done more cheaply at home: "When garments were looking tired we used to dye them with Drummer dyes which were about 1½d. each", even though this involved an element of risk: "I seem to remember I dyed something yellow, and it didn't turn out right so I didn't wear it."

Home-made dyes were even more unpredictable:

"We could only buy white ankle socks so to make a change we used to dye them — for pink ones we used cochineal cake colouring and for blue ones we diluted blue-black ink. They always turned out streaky and sometimes the colour came out on our feet."

It might be supposed that women would feel resentment or anger at the restrictions placed on their freedom to choose and buy clothes. However, this does not seem to have been the case. Several women have pointed out that they had never been able to spend lavishly, and the onset of 'official' austerity did not therefore mark a great change for them.

"We never had a lot ... no, we never had a lot of clothes."

"I was young enough when it started – I was fifteen and I hadn't had a lot ... I don't think we did resent it."

Others briskly relegated fashion to the back of their minds –

"There were more important things to worry about than what you were going to wear tomorrow" –

or accepted the inevitable without fuss:

"You just accepted you couldn't have clothes ... it was amazing really, when you look back, how we did accept things without question, didn't we?"

"The main thing was winning the war and getting it over and all the men back and everyone getting on with a decent life again, so you didn't worry [about clothes]. It was like a trifle really, that was..."

It was a trifle that taxed women's patience and ingenuity, particularly as the war progressed. The queue became a feature of life in the High Street:

"... if you saw a queue you would stand in it just in case there was something going and often you didn't know what you were queuing for."

"In the Stratford Market, there was a woman there, she used to sell all sorts of odds and ends – pins and buttons and elastic and combs – and I used to come in on my day off and queue to get girls [i.e. from a Land Army hostel] combs and knicker elastic and things like that. 'Are you going to Stratford?' they used to say. 'Bring me a comb', 'and me', 'and me' – I used to get about six combs."

For items unobtainable from conventional sources of supply, you could resort to the black market:

"There was a lot of black market – under the counter – going on."

"I used to get the impression that a lot of black market went on – silk undies, etc."

Women could no longer expect to renew garments simply because they had grown tired of them. Clothing had to last.

"Thinking back, we made our things last much longer and you didn't get this colossal change of fashion."

"For a few years I seemed to wear the same clothes – summer and winter. Living in the country we didn't get about much, so maybe no one noticed, though maybe the others in the village were as badly off as we were."

Yet many women are adamant that they managed to maintain a certain standard of dress in spite of shortages and restrictions.

Members of one Women's Institute have written:

"We would like to emphasize to you that all was not doom and gloom. Family and friends co-operated in making and re-making and we certainly do not remember that we looked scruffy all through the war."

Other women make a similar point:

"We kept up appearances, no doubt about that."

"I never remember being untidily or shabbily dressed."

Possibly women living or working in large cities came under greater pressure to be smart, or had more opportunity to be so. One woman recalls that in a Warwickshire Land Army hostel:

"... the London girls were always very smart. They seemed to get — I don't know why — better things than us when they used to go home for week-ends..."

"... going to town every day to work in an office where you were coming into contact with other people, you did make an effort — you had to make an effort."

Although women feel that they 'kept up appearances', some recognize that certain formalities of dress did relax during the war years.

"When I started working in London you went wearing gloves and a hat, matching shoes and a handbag — very formal."

This formality could not be sustained. Hats, although unrationed, became scarcer and more costly and in time disappeared from many heads, to be replaced by the ubiquitous headscarf. Gloves, which were on coupons, were another item previously regarded as essential which could now be dispensed with. This was deplored in some quarters.

"A friend who attended a convent school tells of the horror of a French nun to find that her pupils were proposing to present flowers to a visiting Mother Superior without wearing gloves, as they couldn't spare coupons to buy them. 'You cannot give flowers with your bare hands! It is not nice. It is horrible,' she wailed."

An office worker writes:

"In pre-war days the young men wore black jackets and black and white pin-striped trousers, and the ladies had to wear stockings as slacks were not allowed. Obviously it was not long before these rules had to be abandoned as stockings were in very short supply ... so in summer, the girls were allowed to go without stockings."

Legs, while bare of stockings, were now more frequently covered by trousers. Such garments were practical for war work and nightly dashes to cellar or air-raid shelter as the sirens sounded:

"Before the war I don't remember seeing any lady wearing trousers, but it became the usual dress for most young women. Girls went on the buses, having to run up and down the stairs. Girls on the land and in factories needed sensible dress."

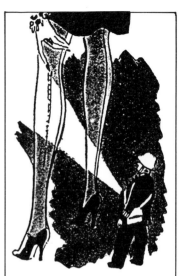

Early to bed... early to rise

EARLY to bed, in a luxurious manner! The chances are you're working hard enough to deserve it. This lovely bed-jacket and hot-water-bottle cover will give that final, comforting touch. A pre-war evening coat or frock in a fairly solid material, such as satin, moiré or taffeta, could be very easily altered to make these.

When making the bed-jacket, use the evening dress material double. And for comfort's sake you might salvage some woollies — say undies that really have served their turn — and use these as a warm inter-lining for shoulders and sleeves.

The smallest scraps of silk left over can be joined to make a very smart topcoat for the hot-water bottle.

Now that there's no Lux, you'll have to take extra care when washing fine things. Rinse well, or specks of undissolved soap may stick to fibres.

Wartime Clothes Service by the LUX *News Scout*

LEVER BROTHERS, PORT SUNLIGHT, LIMITED

1X 2823-96

There was a brief fashion for ankle socks.

"Before the war every Sunday you dressed up — you wouldn't go out unless you were completely dressed up — your handbag and your brolly and your hat and everything to match. [The war] was when they started to get casual ... you had to wear what you could get. That was when women started wearing trousers really, there weren't many slacks worn before the war — it wasn't the done thing."

Formal evening dress was also adapted to meet the changing conditions of life on the Home Front. Lavish frocks were no longer felt to be suitable or appropriate, and women who continued to lead a social life often attended functions in a simple evening skirt and blouse, or a day dress. There were not coupons to spare for frivolous garments.

"You didn't have a choice because of either lack of coupons or lack of money during the war, so your choices were always restricted ... so you didn't have very many frivolous clothes ... the formalities changed."

Anyone in possession of pre-war evening dresses may have worn them through the early years of the war, but by the mid-Forties most had resignedly converted them into something more useful:

"Materials were on coupons, and if you needed a nightdress you saved your coupons by wearing your old evening dresses."

One shortage still remembered vividly, and with humour, is that of fine stockings. Before the war stockings were easily obtainable – "Stockings for 9d. from the market; Woolworth's 6d. a leg!" – but after the outbreak of hostilities the production of silk stockings ceased.

"In the early days of the war, lisle stockings, or rayon, were the order of the day when available and as far as I can remember nylons didn't become available until the latter end of the war."

Until 1946, when production of nylons began here, their availability depended on the generosity of American servicemen who dispensed them, along with chocolate and gum, to a grateful population. As stockings cost coupons, and thick lisle was not comfortable for summer wear, many young women abandoned stockings altogether and went bare-legged during the warm weather. To simulate the appearance of stockings they went to considerable lengths:

"Some girls used Miners liquid make-up in the summer, smearing on this tan or beige dye and getting a friend to draw a seam down the back with an eyebrow pencil."

For this activity "you needed a very steady hand – you had someone else to help you to do it", and "… it was the devil's own job to get it even."

There were unorthodox alternatives to leg make-up: they included gravy browning, cocoa and sand.

"We girls used to 'sand our legs' – apply a paste of sand and water, then draw a line up in pencil."

"I used to wash my legs with sand to give them some colour, then draw a line with soft crayon up the back for the seam."

Ex-land girls remember with some hilarity that their return journeys from work would frequently be punctuated by quests for sand. On spotting an unguarded heap by the roadside, they would bang on the sides of the truck for the driver to stop. Leaping from the vehicle, the girls would scoop small quantities of sand into headscarves, quickly removed for the purpose, before resuming their journey, leaving a bemused pedestrian or two in their wake.

Two reasons are given for this painting of the legs, complete with seam lines. One is that it was not acceptable to be seen publicly without stockings.

"When the war came and stockings were scarce it was embarrassing to go without. This was when girls started to brown their legs and draw black lines up the back to look like stockings."

"I think it was probably the fact that in those days you didn't go without stockings."

Others dispute this and think bare legs became perfectly respectable. They believe women used make-up or sand simply because they disliked appearing with pale legs.

"I don't think it was so much that you were imitating stockings; it was always the thing to have brown legs and the slightest bit of sunshine — up went your skirt and out went your legs to get them brown."

There was a brief fashion for ankle socks, encouraged by magazines such as *Vogue*, although few women remember wearing them:

"I was one of the few who adopted it, wearing scarlet half hose with a navy coat, hat and shoes."

Women spent a considerable amount of time and effort on the purchasing and careful maintenance of stockings.

"… at the market they used to have great big piles of reject stockings from the factories and if you had enough time and patience you might find a pair the same colour — they might not necessarily be the same length — but you could buy them for about 2d. a pair … everybody used to go for them."

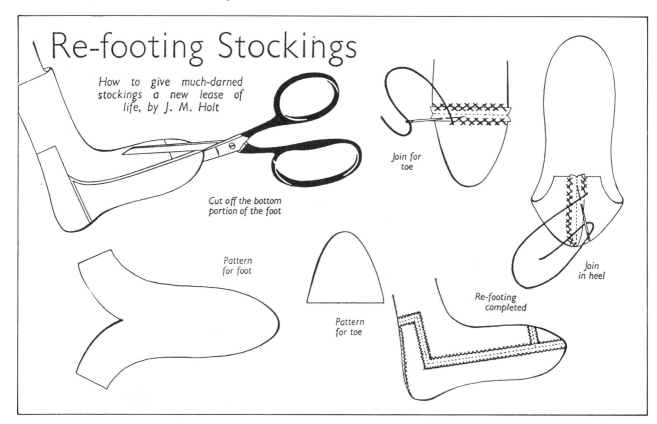

Re-footing Stockings

How to give much-darned stockings a new lease of life, by J. M. Holt

Cut off the bottom portion of the foot

Join for toe

Pattern for foot

Pattern for toe

Join in heel

Re-footing completed

Odd stockings were saved and dyed to match up with others in order to make new pairs.

"We used to dye — even with old tea bags, or tea leaves it was then — put them in muslin bags and put them in water and if you wanted to change the colour of stockings as long as you put them in cold water and brought them up to the boil ... you could bring them up to what colour you wanted them..."

"You'd get them more or less the same colour and you'd put them in a saucepan, bring it to the boil and boil them and keep fetching them out ... and when they all looked the same you'd rinse them off and pair them up..."

Laddered or torn stockings were not discarded. If you lacked the time or expertise to mend them at home, they could be sent out to be professionally repaired. Department stores offered this service.

"We wore lisle stockings and rayon ... they used to wear well ... I can remember darning them ... if they got ladders I remember there were places in the town where you could get them mended — people mended them with a hook..."

Individuals also did repairs at home:

"[they] set up in business repairing stockings and they had a minute little crochet hook and they used to repair ladders for so much a length."

One woman remembers setting up in business in this way, but found she could not continue in it for long:

"I used to do invisible mending on ladders. I think I charged 6d. an inch. I used a needle which was something like a rug hook but very fine. I always had plenty of trade, but stopped doing this when it became a strain on my eyes."

While rationing imposed restrictions on the consumer, the manufacturers of clothing were also subject to government control. In June 1941 the Board of Trade introduced the Utility Scheme for retail goods, including clothing. Utility goods, bearing their distinctive label,

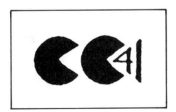

had to meet certain standards and were sold at controlled prices. The aim was to obtain the greatest possible production from limited resources and keep costs to a minimum by simplifying design. Utility garments were therefore practical rather than exciting, and if the fabric was generally satisfactory in quality the hems and seams were minimal in order to avoid waste. Feature

Utility clothes on display.

writers on magazines and newspapers endeavoured to be positive, and their articles pointed out the benefits of Utility ranges:

'From now on we are going to wear Utility clothes. Not because we are burning with a desire to show our patriotism, but just because Utility clothes are the best value on the market today. The materials are far, far better than those shown in garments at a much higher price.'

Generally women remember Utility clothes as being dull but good value for money. Only one expressed real enthusiasm, and this was because her natural preference was for plain tailored styles. The usual reaction is represented by the following comments:

"Utility clothes were made to last ... I can remember having a tweed suit — inverted pleat front and back — worn with knitted jumpers underneath ... and I don't think the quality was any less good. It was a little uninteresting in design, I suppose ... very simple in design. You wouldn't get fancy buttons, it would all be very austere."

"As far as I can remember, the quality was very good ... and I think they were cheaper."

"Utility clothing and furniture were surprisingly well designed, using the simplest of styles and economical materials."

"I had Utility clothes towards the end of the war ... there were different signs on the garments as to how much you had to pay — to stop the profiteering ... They were quite good — oh yes, they were very good really — a lot better than some of the rubbish you could get in the shops."

The government approached a number of leading couturiers and asked them to design a basic Utility range suitable for mass production. Molyneux, Hardy Amies, Digby Morton, Bianca Mosca, Peter Russell and Worth collaborated to produce patterns for top-coat, suit and dresses and these appeared in the shops towards the end of 1942. Reviews were detailed and often favourable:

'Utility suits are extremely good value, cost just under £5 and come in all kinds of dog-tooth checks, in sober plaids, in Glen checks and plain Cheviot tweeds.'

(*Homes and Gardens*, September 1942)

As manufacturers were obliged to devote 85 per cent of their production to Utility clothes, this is what most women bought when they went shopping for a new coat or dress. However, the remaining 15 per cent of their output was not subject to Utility restrictions and this did allow a little scope for the designers and producers of clothes to exercise their creativity. These 'free' clothes were not exempt from purchase tax and were not sold at controlled prices, but were nevertheless much in demand by those who could afford them.

From 1942 the manufacture of clothing was further limited by the Making of Clothes (Restrictions) Orders. As the war progressed, the government felt it necessary to prohibit the use of all superfluous material and labour in the making of clothes. The new restrictions curtailed the use of trimmings and embroidery, specified the maximum length and width of skirts and restricted the number of pleats and amounts of fabric used in each garment.

"Utility clothes were made to last..."

'Celanese' makes the BEST of Utility

War has stripped fashion of "frills and furbelows". But war cannot take away from women their love of beautiful things. Happily this desire for beauty can still be satisfied by Lingerie in 'Celanese'. For, though restrictions ban lace and embroidery, the 'Celanese' Fabrics are still very lovely.

The dictation of fashion by government decree was a unique step, as *Vogue* magazine explained to its readers:

'... what has happened is something new in fashion history. The government has taken a hand in design ... they are only concerned in making economies in fabric and labour — so the restrictions are framed on the one hand to prohibit designs that cut into fabric wastefully; and on the other to eliminate labour-absorbing details and decoration.'

(June 1942)

The effect on women's dress was to make it severe in appearance and practical in design. Stitching, seaming, buttons and pockets were for use rather than decoration and the elimination of trimmings and other unnecessary detail gave coats and suits a military air. As women had accepted rationing, so they now tolerated austerity:

'... thinking back to it, it was life and that's how it was and you didn't question it — there was no choice. You didn't think 'Why is this terribly masculine?' — because it was — it was the style that was on offer and that was that."

Some fashion writers considered restriction to be a good discipline for designers:

'Curbed in many directions, and unable to indulge in an orgy of pockets and pleats, they are discovering a new beauty in austere lines and the drama of unexpected colour combinations.'

(*Homes and Gardens*, September 1942)

The stripping away of 'frills and furbelows', while perhaps deplored by some women, did have a positive side. Poor fabric and bad workmanship could no longer be camouflaged by an excess of fussy trimming, and this helped to improve quality at the cheaper end of the market. Besides becoming simpler, women's clothes became shorter:

"I had two edge-to-edge coats in the forties. These were economical on material, and the tie belts meant that buttons and buckles were not required. Skirt lengths were knee length, again to save material."

Priorities when choosing clothes changed to fit the times. Women had to buy clothes and shoes that were not only practical and hard wearing but also adaptable. One outfit had to serve many purposes, and for this reason plain frocks and pinafore dresses became extremely popular because their appearance could be altered by using them with different accessories:

"You went to work wearing something different most days, even with austerity ... once you'd got a basic, which was my pinafore dress ... that meant you could ring the changes. I know I never went to work in the same thing two days running."

"... a basic dress — dressed up ... little white collars, a white lace collar over a plain dress..."

Picture Post made this point to its readers:

'... If you turn up the fashion magazines of 1939, you'll see how styles have simplified; how shoes, hats, fabrics, have turned from pretty to practical; how extravagances have disappeared altogether.'

(29th August 1942)

One woman felt that the austerity of wartime gave women new freedoms in dress:

"I think it gave them much more freedom ... freedom to wear clothes that were suitable for the times..."

Amongst the 'new freedoms' she included the wearing of trousers and abandoning of stockings, although she recognized that such liberation did not extend to all. The war changed dress,

"... but not for all generations ... my mother was still young enough to have to go to work and she had to go to work in a chemical factory ... but she didn't wear trousers to go there. She wore an ordinary summer dress in the summer, a skirt and knitted jumper in the winter and a wrapover overall ... I never saw her without stockings or wearing trousers."

Vogue magazine summed up the look that was 'suitable for the times'.

'It's a look that does not jar with uniform – with women's uniform ... the eye unconsciously measures women up by this yardstick. Why does that shoulder mane seem so out of date? Because it would look messy hanging on a uniform collar. What's wrong with those exquisite tapered nails? They couldn't do a hand's turn without breaking. The woman who could change instantly into uniform or munitions overall and look charming, soignée and right, is the smart woman of today.'

(January 1942)

In their utilitarian outfits, regulated by government even down to the number of buttons per jacket, did women present a picture of uniform drabness? Old snapshots and documentary photographs seem sometimes to suggest this, but they are usually in black and white and give no idea of the vivid colours worn in wartime. Bright colour, and unexpected colour combinations, enlivened garments that were austere in design. Dresses were often made up in two colours, or from two fabrics, with startling results:

'There are brown frocks with tomato fronts, pale blue fronts, or gold brocade fronts, black with cherry or emerald, tweed dresses with knitted fronts or knitted sleeves or yokes.'

(*Homes and Gardens*, September 1942)

Airforce blue became a popular shade, but the reasons for choosing it sometimes extended beyond merely preferring it to other colours:

"I remember seeing it on a model in the window and thinking 'That is me' – and I went in, tried it on and thought 'Yes, that is it.'
  'The hat actually was a disaster. It was an airforce shape with streamers down the back ... but the material covering the base was crêpe de chine so of course the first shower that I went out in the hat just disintegrated ... On the front I've got an aeroplane (brooch) ... my husband's brother had just been reported missing over the North Sea and he was a pilot in the Air Force ... it was respect for F___ that I had that outfit, yes."

Fabric itself, as well as its colour, could sometimes relieve a severe style. One woman recalls a dress of:

"a crêpe type of material which was very popular but quite soft and feminine..."

It was made up in dark and light blue:

"... in the manufacture of it they'd used all the extra bits and there was a 'V' type belt and that was a very feminine dress."

If manufactured garments had to be functional rather than decorative, it was possible to bring a touch of individuality to dress by making clothes at home, where you were not subject to government controls over pleats and pockets. The war introduced many women to the joys, and perils, of home dressmaking and the results of their labours often ensured that they were uniquely clad!

Economies in fabric and labour led to severely tailored styles.

2 'Make-do-and-mend'

'Make-do-and-mend' is a phrase that seems to trigger instant recall amongst those who remember the Forties. Most women can remember patching, darning, renovating and repairing, and fashioning new garments from the most unlikely fabric and materials.

Rationing had already limited opportunities for the purchase of new clothes. The government's 'Make-do-and-mend' campaign sought to encourage women to mend and adapt clothing they already had, or, as the Board of Trade's advertisements rather snappily put it: "Mend and Make do, To save buying new."

This concept was hardly a novelty for many women; those struggling to raise families on low incomes had been making do and mending for years. But the war extended this to women who, while not previously careless with clothes, had always been able to discard garments when they were dated or worn and buy new ones. Patches and darns were no longer the badge of the disadvantaged, and by 1942 even the glossiest of the fashion magazines were writing that 'dressiness' was outdated.

There was plenty of help and advice available for those who lacked the necessary sewing skills. The Board of Trade produced numerous advertisements, and it was impossible to open a magazine without coming across the beaming features of 'Mrs. Sew-and-Sew'. She was a cartoon character, always cheerful and competent, who told readers how to hem stockinette vests or mend three-cornered tears. These advertisements also urged women to join a sewing class, of which hundreds sprang up all over the country. Many took advantage of them:

"We made a great effort to repair and remake and actually enjoyed it. W.V.S. ran 'Make-do-and-mend' groups which were very sociable occasions."

Many local groups, including Women's Institutes, held sessions on clothing repair and renovation as part of their programme of talks and activities.

Publishers produced books with titles like *New Clothes from Old*, and magazines ran regular features to inspire those who had run out of ideas:

"I have a book that I bought about 1942 which tells how to make-do-and-mend. Making two jumpers out of three, etc. Everyone had to mend in those days."

Some young women were fortunate in having mothers, or other close female relatives, who

---

'Talk on Dress Renovation at Shipston on Stour'

Miss Coleman presided at the monthly meeting of Shipston-on-Stour Women's Institute, held in the hostel.

A talk was given by Mrs. Cutts, of Chipping Campden, on dress renovations and alterations which was particularly helpful and interesting in these times.

(*Stratford Herald*, 23rd October 1942)

were able seamstresses. They would either sew for their daughters, or teach them how to do it for themselves:

"Our generation seem to have had mothers who were good needlewomen."

"There was a lot of 'Make-do-and-mend' ... my mother was very clever at sewing, she made me lots of nice things."

"My mother, having five children, and step-children, always had to spend carefully and was always on the look-out for remnants of material. When war came, she was lucky for she had a trunk full. She had always made our dresses but only when we were growing out of what we were wearing. These remnants were a godsend during those war years, for the only dresses I had were made from those materials. Sometimes a contrasting colour had to be used for collars, cuffs, even yokes."

If you had no relative to help, but had a little cash to spare, you could either call on the services of a local dressmaker – "Use in those days was made much more of people who could sew ... you didn't necessarily go and buy a frock" – or, in the last resort, teach yourself to sew:

"We always had to 'Make-do-and-mend' to supplement our clothing coupons, and my very first dressmaking effort was making my son his first little suit from my mother's red woollen swim suit! Nothing was ever thrown away in the clothes line until it had been utilized over and over again."

"My husband went to a sale and returned with a German sewing machine. The machine worked and we found a Singer machine needle to fit it. I bought a book of 'make-do-and-mend' for one shilling. Up to this time, since leaving school, my sewing had been limited to sewing on buttons and shoulder straps ... The machine was a real treasure – on it I made curtains, the children's clothes, even top-coats and my own dresses ... the machine was in use for some twenty years till the type of needle was discontinued by Singers ... I can only recall one disaster, when we cut out two left fronts to a coat we had unpicked and reversed."

What did 'Make-do-and-mend' mean in practice? It was not sewing as a hobby – a relaxing pastime to while away the odd leisure hour or two. It became a necessity, and while some women may have enjoyed the challenges it presented, for others it was an arduous chore that had to be slotted into an already busy working life. Besides repair and renovation, it included home dressmaking. Those able to sew, or willing to try, could buy pattern and fabric and make garments at home. Such clothes were free from the restrictions binding commercial manufacturers. However, material by the yard cost coupons, and it was not always possible to find something suitable: "You could get it, but it wasn't always what you wanted."

Women with male friends and relatives in the services could sometimes acquire fabric from overseas.

"The real solution was to have brothers, husband or boyfriends from or posted to America, Canada, Australia, etc. as they could bring or send clothing or materials – even post parcels home."

"… that was material brought back … from abroad and I had a coat and skirt made out of it. My husband brought it back from abroad … this was when he was in the navy – he brought a lot of stuff back for me."

"I could tell you a tale about my cousin. Her husband was a vicar – or a padre then, as they called them – and he was in Burma and after they surrendered … he brought trunks and trunks back with beautiful lace and materials – silks and things from Burma. You know, they have lovely things there – and carpets as well he brought back … I think she made all her clothes and then a bit later on she had a little girl and she made all the things for her. Oh yes, they brought a lot of things back."

Not everyone was in the happy position of receiving trunks from Burma. As the war progressed, women began to turn to unrationed sources of fabric in order to save precious coupons, and found themselves making garments from material they would never have dreamt of using otherwise: "I didn't resort to having anything made out of a blanket but lots of people did…"

Winter coat made from a blanket.

ISSUED BY THE BOARD OF TRADE

Which stitch?

says Mrs. SEW-and-SEW

When you're making a new garment out of an old one so much depends on knowing the right way to stitch your hems and seams. So here's a simple general knowledge test. If you don't know the answers, a Make-Do and Mend Class will help you.

What's the right seam for children's knickers or overalls?

WRONG! French seam. Clumsy for strong materials — bulky and difficult to handle at crutch. RIGHT! Run and fell seam. Tack one raw edge ¼" above the other on the wrong side. Machine ⅛" below lower edge. Turn upper edge over ¼". Open out seam so that the hem lies flat. Tack and hem (Diagram B).

How would you hem a thick cloth coat or stockinette vest?

WRONG! Turned-in machine hem. It's too bulky and too rigid RIGHT! Single turn of stuff— herringbone-stitched (Diagram A). Makes nice flat hem which 'gives' to fabric.

A SURE WAY TO SAVE COUPONS!

Join a Make-Do and Mend Class and get expert help with your sewing difficulties. Your local Evening Institute, Technical College or Women's Organisation, is probably running a class. Or ask your Citizens' Advice Bureau.

'Lots of people' certainly did use blankets, and transformed them into top-coats and jackets for winter wear. If well-made, they could be a very acceptable substitute for coats made from more orthodox materials.

"My own mother made coats for all the girls in the family and for herself too, but these coats were made from blankets. Some of them were cream but mine was a grey one and to my mind this looked less like a blanket than the cream ones."

"It was airforce blue and I believe it was lined – I have a feeling we had something we used as the lining because otherwise it would have been very rough. It was very useful and very warm of course – lovely."

This particular blanket coat was worn with a navy blue duster as a headscarf, which "fortunately went rather well with the coat … anything that could be used we made use of."

Curtains, and particularly curtains of a luxurious fabric like velvet, could be made into dresses for special occasions:

"Curtains we used … velvet curtains we made into clothes. If anyone had velvet curtains they were used."

"We used to use curtains that were left off."

After the war ended and the black-out was lifted, householders were no longer obliged to darken their windows at night. Black curtain fabric could then be put to alternative uses:

"You could buy black-out material. It was just a twill – various widths – I remember I bought some."

One woman employed a local dressmaker to sew items for her trousseau:

"She was very clever this lady – she made me a housecoat out of black-out material, which was a fine – well, a fine lining, I suppose, with a sheen on it – and it was a classic gored style and she appliquéd up each panel cut-outs of flowers, on the eight gores."

Such a garment may not have been luxurious but it was certainly unique: no one else would have had one quite like it, and it supports the claim that "Anybody with any imagination could make all sorts of things."

Certainly it took imagination to see the fashion potential in a draughtsman's discarded plans. These drawings, on tracing linen, could be salvaged and recycled into useful, coupon-free fabric.

"If you were lucky enough to know a draughtsman, you would beg him to give you his old drawings, so that you could boil them and get a fine cambric material from them which you could make into handkerchiefs or brassieres. You did not have tissues for noses in those days."

One woman still has a petticoat – lace trimmed, in a fine white cotton – that she made in this way. Working in a planning office she was, on occasion, able to take old plans home and convert the stiff linen, with its bluish tinge, into a usable fabric.

Several women remember transforming large food and flour bags into a material which could be made up into items of household linen such as pillow cases and table napkins, or garments like skirts:

"You could get flour bags from the mills and we used to boil them, bleach them — they were coarse but they were thick cotton and quite nice."

"Cotton dress material must have been available as I made at least two sun dresses, which I wore with short, white bolero-style jackets. One of these I made from a flour bag begged from the grocer, and another from two tea towels. I had another one in a pink woollen material which, I think, was originally part of a baby's blanket."

Butter muslin, with its gauzy open weave, was unrationed and therefore much sought after:

"Mothers were allowed to buy butter muslin to use as additional napkins, the terry nappies were part of the clothing coupon allowance but the muslin was 'coupon-free'. Very rarely was the muslin used for nappies..."

"I had been used to making my own [clothes] but as time went on things were more difficult and I had to search around — butter muslin was not on points, so that made nightdresses, dusters, dish cloths, etc."

Parachutes, complete or in portions, seem to have been one fabric source that all women remember using. Silk and nylon parachutes, made up in long triangular sections, could be unpicked and reused for knickers, nightdresses, petticoats and brassieres. Silk was preferred to nylon — it was pleasanter to wear next to the skin than the clammy, slippery nylon, and was an easier fabric to stitch. Women are a little vague about how they got hold of parachutes during the war itself:

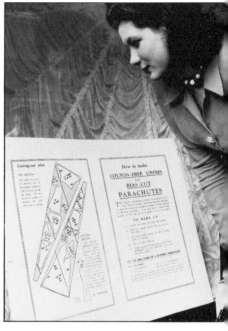

Shop window display featuring a parachute, with directions for 'coupon-free undies'.

"There was a lot of black market. You could get things like parachutes and we made underwear — you could make lovely underwear if you had the time to do it."

"When the war had been on a bit, we used to rush off to Birmingham to buy nylon or silk parachutes (if we were lucky) to make knickers and underslips from. As these were on the cross, we had to have special patterns for these items."

One way of obtaining parachutes was to work in the factories that produced them, or to know someone who did:

"During the war I worked as a machinist making army uniforms, and the main item, parachutes. These varied in size from very small ones used to parachute pigeons behind enemy lines to the very large ones. The larger they were the more we wanted to work on them because if there was a flawed panel or half panel, after long negotiations the machinist was allowed to keep it. Hence all my pants, bras, petticoats and blouses during the war were made of parachute silk."

Parachute underwear could be trimmed with oddments of lace and ribbon, or embroidered, to give a touch of individuality lacking in the flesh-pink Utility ranges available in shops. However, not all parachute fabric warranted such attention:

"I've just remembered the nylon parachutes, in the most awful colours, that we sometimes managed to get to be cut up for all sorts of things."

LOUNGE SUIT INTO COSTUME

A man's discarded lounge suit can be converted into a woman's costume. Remove the jacket lining, unpick all seams, then press the material flat under a damp cloth. The jacket is recut in sections as much the same lines as before. Diagrams 2 and 3. As the material is reversed, the original buttonholes will not present difficulties by being on the wrong side

FRONT   BACK

2

FRONT SKIRT   BACK SKIRT

UNDER SLEEVE   UPPER SLEEVE

3

BINDING

Instructions for making the jacket pattern from the block pattern will be found on page 130, while the skirt pattern should be prepared from the skirt block on page 54. The skirt is cut in four sections from the trouser legs as shown in the Diagram 1 on the left.

FROM AN OLD COAT

Girl's Coat

Gas Mask Carrier

Lady's Dress

Odd Skirt

Kettle Holders

Odd Jacket

COMBINING GARMENTS

From 1945 parachutes were on open sale, and could be bought from many stores. Instructions were also provided, and according to one shop-window sign, 'out of one-third of a 24-panel parachute you can make two nightdresses, two slips, two pairs of cami-knickers, and four pairs of knickers'.

"A Dutch college friend of mine married in Holland just after the war and asked me to make her a nightdress for her trousseau as a wedding present. She told me exactly what she wanted (which was rather simpler than I would have chosen!) – quite plain but edged round neck and arm holes with lace. I made the nightdress from a pure silk parachute. The government was selling parachutes off just after the war and we bought them to make underwear, as one did not have to use clothing coupons to buy parachutes whereas one did to buy material by the yard. The sections, when unpicked, were quite big though I may have had to 'graft' a piece on to get the size needed for the nightdress skirt."

The same woman was able to acquire 'little' parachutes from her brother:

"… my brother was attached to a parachute Regimental Research Station on Salisbury Plain. There they were researching using *little* (about 2 ft or 2 ft 6in. in diameter) parachutes. These were made of a fine cotton. After an 'experiment' was over there were a number of these cotton parachutes scattered over the plain and my brother retrieved quite a few. They were useful as coupon-free hankies, or, pieced together, to make into knickers, etc."

As well as sewing clothes from whatever materials came to hand, 'Make-do-and-mend' also involved adapting existing garments to make new ones. Evening dresses and other seldom-worn clothes were soon transformed into something more useful, but as everyday garments became worn they were also cut up, cut down, or combined with serviceable parts of other clothing to produce something wearable.

"It was amazing how clothes were cut down and remade. Nothing was wasted at all."

"There was a lot of making-do and changing round the things you had."

Coats proved extremely versatile, and magazines provided advice and ideas on how they could be utilized:

"We used to make old coats into coat dresses … and skirts – we cut the bottom off of a coat to make a skirt, you know.".

"We made skirts from old coats."

Dresses frequently wore first at the armhole, neck and wrist and these areas could be cut away and replaced by remnants, or fabric taken from good parts of another dress. A stain or tear could be cut away completely, being replaced by a panel or band of contrasting fabric:

"[I] bought remnants when I could find any and with the best parts of old dresses made up new ones with gores or bands of the remnants."

If a male relative could be persuaded to part with a suit, this could be cut down into women's or children's clothes. One wonders whether many servicemen returned from the war to find their

"That skirt is my new husband's sailor whites..."

civilian jackets and trousers no longer in their wardrobes but on their wives. Certainly their serv
uniforms did not remain intact for long once the men had been demobbed:

"That skirt is my new husband's sailor whites — that's what they called their trousers that t
wore abroad — and that skirt was made out of it. I didn't make it but I think I may have put
braid round and I also have a picture of myself somewhere wearing his navy trousers made .
a pinafore dress."

Other items were removed from men's wardrobes and modified for wear by wives a
daughters. One woman remembers an entire 'Make-do-and-mend' outfit, worn to greet
husband on one of his rare visits home on leave:

"I met him at the station in his pants (a bit of lace had made them into knickers), his shirt a
blouse, his pyjama jacket as a blazer and a skirt made from a bleached food stuff bag, and a b
made from cellophane. And he never even noticed."

Another devised an outfit inspired by her husband's military uniform, and which incorpora
one of his shirts:

"For six years my husband was in the Highland Light Infantry, a regiment which wore
Mackenzie tartan, so I sent to House of Fraser in Edinburgh for a length of that tartan in dr
weight. From this I made a circular skirt (although the fashion was really for short, straight ski
with 'braces' ... next I took one of my husband's white shirts and shortened the sleeves. Whe
wore this with the tartan skirt I had a Mackenzie tartan tie, fastened with a brooch in the sha
of the Highland Light Infantry badge. If I wore the top and skirt together as a 'dress' I use
genuine H.L.I. cap badge as a buckle for the belt — probably against all Army regulations!"

Pyjama tops seem to have been popular either as blazers, or, as in this case, blouses:

"I remember going out with my pyjama top on under a costume. I went to meet my friend — s
worked at the Post Office — and she said, 'Oh! D___ has come in her pyjamas!' They w
striped cotton — they were very pretty and I thought, 'Mm, that'd look nice with my navy b
costume.' We did all sorts of things like that."

Besides making and modifying garments for themselves, many women had to provide cloth
for their children, who were often on the receiving end of some very individual outfits:

"When I was confirmed my mother was so worried because we hadn't any clothing coupons
spare for a dress which would only be worn once, even the material to make one would ha
used up precious coupons, so mother racked her brains and came up with the bright idea
using her best pre-war nightdress — a white crêpe silk one. A few tucks and gathers in
appropriate places and a sash made from blue hair ribbon — no one in the church realized I v
being confirmed in a nightie — or I hope they didn't."

"I thought I would like to tell you the tale of the cowgown (a coat used by farmers). My fat
used it until the sleeves were worn away and many darned holes caused by the hed
brambles. I unpicked it and made my toddler some dungarees, covering the darns with w

unpicked from an old jumper and pieces of material from the rag bag. After my daughter got over the crawling stage the knees were unpatchable so I cut them off above the knees and bound them, with more rag bag bits. These were worn until she was four years old and outgrew them. No, that wasn't the end of the shorts as my friend's toddler wore them for another two years. By the time they went into the rag bag there was more patch than cowgown. We were sorry to say goodbye after seven years of useful service."

Perhaps the most laborious aspect of 'Make-do-and-mend' was the repair of garments that had seen better days. As nothing was thrown away, whenever fabric wore thin or holes appeared women took out needle and thread in order to patch and darn:

"We spent our evenings darning our stockings and mending our clothes whilst we listened to the radio."

"Mending took up a lot of women's spare time, and a patch was an honourable badge in those days."

From applying small patches and repairing tears, some women went to great lengths to salvage shabby clothes. 'Turning', or unpicking an item and remaking it on the wrong side, was not to be undertaken lightly and even women's magazines were a little hesitant about recommending it wholeheartedly. All linings, fastenings and trimmings had to be unpicked, removed and safely stored. All seams were then unstitched, and the pieces of fabric that had once been a coat or dress were washed or dry cleaned. Sometimes recutting was necessary in order to remove weak or worn patches before the garments could be remade with the unworn, unfaded 'inside' now being uppermost. This operation was tedious and time-consuming, and unless the garment was of good quality cloth, the finished product could be disappointing.

Many women could knit and were used to producing jumpers and cardigans at home. However, as new wool was rationed and women could not always spare coupons to buy it, they had to unravel and reknit existing garments to make new ones:

"A lot of knitting was done by unravelling old knitted garments. We even knitted our stockings, if we were fortunate enough to find some knitting cotton. Before the war you could knit a jumper with four ounces of wool at 6d. per ounce. Wool was quite fine in those days, before double knitting was invented."

Wool producers continued to advertise their products although they were often in short supply. Some advertisements contributed to the 'Make-do-and-mend' campaign by giving suggestions for 'coupon-free knitting', while ensuring that their brand name remained in the public eye. One advertiser included 'a sense of adventure' amongst the materials required for remaking a jumper, but perhaps should also have added 'endless patience' and 'plenty of spare time'.

"1 lb knitting wool made a twin set, with some over to help out when the whole lot were unknitted and remade. When elbows wore thin sleeves were changed over so that the darned thin part was on the inside of the bend. Sleeves knitted from the top were easier to unknit *in situ*."

Outfit in Mackenzie tartan, uniform of the Highland Light Infantry.

RULES
FOR
RAYON

RAYON is a wonderful fabric, but it needs knowing if you are to get the best out of it. *Though flexible and hard wearing when dry, it temporarily loses almost half of its strength when wet.* So when you are washing rayon things handle them tenderly. Don't soak them—dip them. Don't boil them—use lukewarm water. Never wring or twist them.

When you hang them up to dry hang them evenly so that they do not pull out of shape.

IRON SPEAKING

" I like to smooth things out, you know, so perhaps you'll allow me to give you a few hints. ‣ First remember that rayons can't stand too much heat. Try me on a pad of paper. If I'm too hot, a scorch mark will show in 20 seconds. Rayon fabrics should be ironed on the ' wrong ' side and you should always press one thickness at a time to avoid creases. Lock-knit fabrics should be ironed *across* the weave to prevent stretching."

HOW TO BLOT OUT THE STAINS

Use two pieces of white blotting paper when you tackle a grease stain on rayon material. Lay it on the lower sheet of blotting paper and apply the stain remover (benzine or similar fluid) all round the spot or stained area. Then press down firmly between the two sheets so that the blotting paper may soak up the dissolved grease and thus remove the stain.

MIND THE LADDER!

Look out for ladders, tears and split seams. If you always keep a needle and cotton handy you can often save a garment by " first-aid " treatment, before the trouble can develop seriously.

Mend and make do
To save buying new

JOIN A MAKE-DO AND MEND CLASS

INSTRUCTIONAL CLASSES and mending parties are being formed all over the country. Already there are hundreds of them in full swing. Any Citizens' Advice Bureau will be glad to tell you where and when your nearest sewing party meets, and how you can join or help to form one in your own district.

ISSUED BY THE BOARD OF TRADE

"My mother produced two pairs of large knitted woollen knickers with legs, but in a lovely shade of blue and of green. Seams unpicked and the gusset area cut away, I used the ribbed top for the hem of two lovely warm jumpers with short sleeves, and an appliqué flower on each front."

Ingenious methods were adopted to minimize the amount of wool needed for a garment:

"We used to knit cravats with a roll collar to tuck into our coats, so that it looked as if we had a jumper on underneath. They were very warm round the neck."

These 'cunning little fronts', as one knitting pattern described them, used far less wool than a complete jumper and could provide variety under a suit that had to be worn regularly. Striped jumpers in bright colours also became popular because they could be knitted up from small quantities of wool that were of little use on their own. Oddments could also be turned into gloves and mittens.

"I remember knitting a pair of woollen mitts and matching pixie hood around 1941. They had a blue background and were covered with hideous pink bobbles."

As with fabric, women sought out unrationed supplies of yarn in order to keep knitting. One woman remembers her mother buying darning wool from Woolworths. This came in short lengths which could be painstakingly joined to knit up into a garment.

"Unrationed dish cloth yarn could be knitted up for vests" and even for home furnishings: "My grandma made net curtains the hard way; she crocheted them from dish cloth cotton — this was also 'coupon-free'."

Taking care of fabrics in order to make them last became particularly important after the outbreak of war. Insect pests and careless laundering could damage clothes, which could then be replaced only with difficulty. Soap packets carried advice on fabric care, and the manufacturers of Oxydol soap included items of 'Make-do-and-mend washday wisdom' in their magazine advertisements. This 'wisdom', dispensed by a character called 'Busy Bubble', placed a heavy emphasis on the use of Oxydol's own granulated soap rather than any particular washing or ironing technique, but is typical of many advertisements that exploited the problems of austerity to promote their products.

The Board of Trade issued less subjective announcements to advise on the correct care of fabrics, particularly synthetics such as rayon, which required tender treatment if it were not to be irreparably spoilt.

'Make-do-and-mend' extended beyond the knee to the foot, where women exercised their imagination to preserve the shoes they had and even to make new ones. Shoes, like clothes, were rationed, and many women tended to buy footwear that was serviceable and suited to a variety of occasions:

"... the style was very basic so one pair of shoes, if properly looked after, probably took you through the war."

Looking after shoes involved regular visits to a cobbler, or doing repairs at home:

CAMOUFLAGE
FOR UNDERARM
SHABBINESS

DOLMAN STRIP

DOLMAN STRIP

An effective method of repairing a dress which has worn thin under the arms, is to introduce curved bands of contrast material right around the armhole. These bands should be 2½ ins. to 3 ins. wide, using the armhole of the block pattern from which to cut your pattern, as you see in the diagram. Tack the cut bands into position, try on the dress, and if the bands set properly, edge stitch round them, preferably by machine, and cut away surplus material from underneath afterwards.

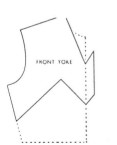

FRONT YOKE

BACK YOKE

Underarm shabbiness is one of the main reasons why a dress has frequently to be discarded before it is truly worn out. This can be avoided by an easy renovation, calling for a small amount of fresh material to be introduced into the dress as if it were part of the design, and not just a patch. This new material must be chosen in a shade that tones or contrasts well. The diagram above illustrates how a vandyked yoke, camouflaging considerable underarm shabbiness, can be cut from the block pattern. The old bodice must be unpicked and the new material cut to shape, and laid over it, then the surplus worn material cut away before the bodice is made up afresh as shown in the sketch on the left.

"Shoes were another problem. The heels and soles were of leather and quickly wore out. Cobblers were hard to come by as most of them had gone to the war. If you were fortunate to find one, it usually took about six weeks to get your repairs done, and lots of us could not spare our shoes that long. I used to repair my friends' shoes overnight, by putting on rubber heels and stick-on rubber soles which we could buy quite cheaply – 1/3d. for the heels and about half a crown for the soles complete with adhesive."

The manufacturers of soles and heels claimed it was 'a national duty' to use them, and advertisements showed how women could be both patriotic and thrifty.

One woman remembers that in pre-war Britain "A super pair of shoes would not cost more than 21/- and crocodile ones were usually about 42/-."

However, after 1939 a shortage of leather meant that not only did prices rise (although Utility shoes sold at a controlled price) but substitute materials had to be found.

"After a time, even leather became very scarce, so we used to wear wooden-sole sandals. These soles were very thick and had a hinge under the instep to make walking more comfortable, but they were rather noisy."

As with fabric, shoes could be brought back from abroad. One woman was given a pair by her fiancé on his return from South Africa: "He brought them back for me to be married in. They were white buckskin, you know, lovely, almost velvety."

Other fiancés, if nearer to home, could make shoes from materials found in shed or workshop:

"I remember R____ made me some shoes because you could buy a wedge-heel base – a sole with this wedge heel and then you could get ... electrician's tape – it was a wide white tape – and so R____ made these shoes which were kind of cross-over straps and it went and tied round and there you had a pair of wedge-heeled shoes ... and they were very very acceptable – they were quite coveted."

For anyone needing shoes of a different colour, a tin of paint came in handy:

"On one occasion, one of my friends wanted a pair of white sandals for summer so I painted white a pair of grey suede sandals she had and surprisingly they wore very well indeed."

Slippers did not have to be hardwearing, and it was often possible to find enough scraps and skill to produce a pair. Few, however, could have been quite so bizarre as a pair described in a letter to *The Land Girl* magazine, and recalled by an ex-member of the Women's Land Army:

"One land girl wrote to say she'd made moleskin slippers: 'First catch your mole, the skin is quite easy to cure, just soak in paraffin and stretch on a board to dry.' There were rat and mole catchers in the Land Army."

For those without access to moles, or furry animals of any kind, slippers could be made from more conventional materials:

"We could get cork wedges which we covered with scraps of material and used old hats to make a very comfortable pair of slippers. We made the soles out of cork inner-soles, and they lasted quite well in the house, but of course, not suitable for outside."

Children's shoes, particularly certain types and makes, could also be in short supply and one woman remembers her long and fruitless wait for sandals:

"Children today take sandals for granted but during the war they were very scarce — the only way one could buy Clarks sandals was by putting your name on a list at one of the larger shoe shops. The waiting list was very long: my name never did come up but my younger brother had his — after a two-year wait."

It might be thought that women had more than enough to do in simply clothing themselves, without worrying about 'Make-do-and-mend' accessories. Yet magazines were full of articles on how to make belts, bags, jewellery and a host of trimmings to brighten dreary wartime wardrobes. These items could be produced from a variety of scraps and natural materials, and some women appear to have dedicated much patience and imagination to making them:

"You had to adapt to what you could get. I made a bag by sewing a 1½in. coarse cotton braid together until it was large enough to make the bag. It worked very well and lasted for years."

One woman has a 'cellophane belt' — a wide piece of braid decorated with a pattern made from tiny squares of folded cellophane, each carefully stitched to the braid. The belt fastens with a pretty buckle removed from an old dress belt.

There were few women who did not have to 'Make-do-and-mend', often at the end of a long working day. As most single women, and many married ones, were engaged in war work the time, effort and imagination spent on extending the life of wartime garments was a considerable achievement.

SOMETHING TO BRIGHTEN IT !

No Matter How Crowded Your Life Is, That Little Dark Frock Must Have A Happy "Lift" of Colour.

shanks as much as possible. Do not draw the thread too tight or the necklace will not hang nicely. Finish off with the same number of beads and the other half of the clasp.

The necklace shown was made of pale coral pink buttons, but white buttons would look equally nice on black. Yellow, blue, dark green, scarlet and mulberry coloured buttons of this kind are also obtainable.

This necklace was made from coral pink, hollow, domed buttons, costing about 11d. a dozen. You will need 6½ dozen buttons, four to six smallish beads, and a clasp or fastener of some kind.

Use strong linen thread double and commence by attaching one-half of the clasp securely at the end of the thread, and then pick up two or three of the beads before you thread on the buttons. These should be bunched round the thread so that they lap over each other and conceal the

Another use for a Buttonhole.

Have you a pretty felt or wool buttonhole which maybe you are tired of using in your coat lapel? Twist up the stems and fix it to the centre of a piece of cord or ribbon, or velvet, with a stitch or two, and wear it round your neck as a necklace.

3 Work

As men left their civilian jobs to serve in the armed forces, their places at work were taken by women. Initially this was a voluntary process: women freely gave up their ordinary employment and went into war work. However, despite a widespread advertising campaign by the Ministry of Labour, not enough volunteered for factory, farm or forces and the government introduced conscription for women in December 1941.

"The call-up for women was under way, and my own age group – those born in 1920 – was the first to register ... For those of us who didn't wish to join the forces there was a wide variety of options ... As a pacifist, I chose the Land Army, but it was full at the time and it was several weeks before I received my papers."

Another woman feels that the choices available were more limited:

"Well, there wasn't much choice really: people who wanted to go in the services were in the services and people like me – they were sent to the nearest factory or whatever where they needed you ... but nobody objected – we'd all been doing things ... I started off with a local relief organization and then I went in the local A.R.P., and then I was conscripted."

By mid 1943, nine out of ten single women under the age of fifty-one and eight out of ten married women were in the forces or industry. The remainder, those classified as 'immobile', were caring for children or dependent relatives but still finding time, in many cases, to do part-time or voluntary work. This mass mobilization of women for the war effort meant that a large number found themselves in unfamiliar places, doing unfamiliar jobs in unfamiliar clothes.

One area of work new to many women was labouring on the land. The Women's Land Army recruited land girls to replace the absent men, and while some were local women many others were drafted in to counties such as Warwickshire from different parts of the country. Most had no experience of farm work, and few had worn the type of clothing with which they were now presented. Newly arrived in a Land Army hostel, one woman remembers unpacking an oilskin bundle containing her uniform:

"There was a fawn drill milking coat and dungarees, two aertex shirts, six pairs of thick woollen socks, canvas gaiters as a substitute for gumboots, and the green jersey and khaki breeches which were the walking-out uniform of the Land Army. I was disappointed to find the greatcoat was missing, and shuddered as I took out the black boots. Would I ever be able to walk in them?"

(Librarian in the Land Army, Dorothea Abbott)

Uniform of the Women's Land Army.

Being provided with a uniform did not exempt land girls from the tedium of darning and mending. Worn garments were replaced only when they were shown to be beyond redemption:

"Socks were re-footed, and Land Army socks had to be darned over and over again before you became eligible for a new pair. One girl sewed little wash leather shields into the toes and heels of hers."

Periodically, official instructions on the care of uniform were received:

"We were told to put a bag of sawdust in our hat to help it keep its shape, and after a day's work in wet weather to stuff our boots with hay and straw. We were told that both boots and shoes would need breaking in and (sternly) that we must not mind if the boots in particular felt hard at first. To which advice we were tempted to reply 'stuff it'."

(Librarian in the Land Army, Dorothea Abbott)

The 'walking-out' or official uniform is remembered with some pride by former land girls:

"We were all proud of our uniform — our proper uniform we walked out in. We liked to go out together in it."

It comprised:

"... corduroy jodphur-type trousers, knee-length woollen stockings pulled right up to your knee and then turned over — you needed a garter to hold them up. Lace-up brown shoes, green jersey — 'V' necked, with a long-sleeved shirt and a tie, and we also had arm bands on our arm — they were green."

Girls were also issued with a top-coat and hat:

"... a heavy top-coat with a slit in the back. It came down to your knees, double breasted. And we wore a felt hat and we all wore them in a different way."

Besides this official uniform, the Land Army also provided working clothes. Young women who had previously worked in shop and office, or been neatly attired in the cap and apron of domestic service, now climbed into dungarees, white aertex blouses and heavy boots:

"We wore those dungarees, and a cowgown. It's like a man's shop overall with a belt on. They're heavy cotton, 'V' necked, with lapels and buttons — and that was only three-quarter length. That's what we wore for work."

For many land girls this was not only their first experience of wearing dungarees, but of being in trousers of any description. Several, who had been brought up in small communities away from large towns or cities, do not remember seeing women in trousers at all before the war but recognized the necessity of wearing them for land work:

"I realized it was practical. We needed to dress like that. Couldn't go out in dresses, could you, doing the jobs we did on the land? I didn't mind at all."

Some land girls took to wearing trousers when off duty:

"I was twenty-two when I bought my first pair of slacks; this was on joining the Land Army, when after wearing breeches or dungarees for work a skirt could seem very cold in the draughty, servants' quarters of the manor we were billeted in."

Others rapidly abandoned them for skirts at the earliest opportunity:

"I couldn't get used to them and I never wore them after. No, I've never worn them since. Don't like them!"

Other women went into industry, and found themselves in factories producing aircraft, munitions and items vital to the war effort. While some women went to work locally, others were sent many miles away to areas of the country that were quite new to them. One woman, from Yorkshire, describes how she ended up in Leamington Spa. Engaged in domestic service, she announced to her employer that she was leaving to do war work:

"She wasn't very pleased, but I went back home to the Labour Exchange and asked them about

Land girls in working clothes.

*"I'd never seen a factory before.
I nearly had a fit."*

it and they sent me to this Technical College for ten weeks training – lathes, they trained us on. When we'd finished the training we had to go back to the Labour Exchange and they gave us a choice – Leamington Spa or Grantham, and we said Leamington Spa. We'd never heard of it – we thought it was the seaside…"

For young women from small communities, whose experience of work had been in shops or domestic service, the huge and noisy factory environment presented an awesome change:

"I'd lived a very quiet life in a village – not a hectic life at all and my mother used to say to me 'You don't know how one half of the world lives', but when I'd been at the factory a week, I said to mother, '*You* don't know how the other half of the world lives either'. It was such a complete change … Oh yes – the conversations – everything was turned into something smutty or suggestive and it was difficult to know what to say … I was very shy, but I must say I came out a very different person!"

"We were homesick for a long time … I was dead quiet, wouldn't say boo to a goose, so I used to get teased a lot."

In spite of training at Technical Colleges and Government Training Centres before beginning factory work, the machines themselves frequently appeared intimidating to the new recruits:

"I'd never seen a factory before. I nearly had a fit. They took us into this one shop first and it was very dark … I thought, 'Oh Lord, I shall never be able to do this – handles and gadgets and everything.' They let you have a go on one, then they put you on your own machine."

In the rush to get women workers into industry some missed their training altogether, with near disastrous results:

"We went in on the first day and they put me on a drilling machine – you can imagine – I'd been a hairdresser and to go into a factory was awful. There was all this noise, machinery, hammering metal – I was taken on to this section and the chap put me on a machine and he said, 'You put this little bit of metal in here and then you pull the handle and drill holes, you see.' So he moved from me to the next one, didn't wait – he was in such a hurry – people wanted planes … I got this and I put it in – I gradually eased it under and pulled the handle down and it immediately disappeared. I went up to the man and said, 'Excuse me, it's gone', and he said, 'What?' and I said, 'I don't know – that thing you gave me', and he said, 'Oh my God!' – bit of language as well – and he looks round and right over the other side of the factory there's somebody holding the jigger, and he said, 'You nearly killed somebody!' He said, 'Do you know anything about drilling?' And I said, 'No, I've never seen a drilling machine before.' And he said, 'What have you been doing?' And I said, 'I was a hairdresser.' And he said, 'Oh my God!'

I worked on those machines for some time. I hated it, but made the best of it."

Besides the initial anxieties presented by a new job in an alien working environment, factory workers found themselves in clothes they had previously seen only on fathers and brothers. One woman, who, as a domestic servant, had worn "… the blue dress and white apron in the morning and you changed in the afternoon to the black dress and little white apron – I wouldn't wear a cap, I hated caps", now put on a boilersuit and heavy shoes to work at her lathe.

Factories seem to have varied in what they expected women workers to wear. Some supplied outfits, so that the workforce was uniformly dressed.

"All of us wore the same — we had brown overalls, they were all the same — we used to pay for them to be laundered at work. Every Thursday they used to come with new clean caps and new clean overalls — they were a sort of gingery brown, quite loose, a tie belt round, which we used to put the ends into the pocket because they were always in the way, and these little hats that came over — like a nurse's cap."

One woman remembers being provided with an all-in-one boilersuit in khaki or navy, and that hair had to be tied back when working near machines.

In other factories, women appear to have provided their own clothes for work. Some photographs show them in skirts and wraparound overalls, but many appear in trousers or

Factory workers in overalls, with tin hats at the ready.

dungarees, often topped with a short and brightly coloured smock. These cotton overalls were applauded in an article in *Housewife* magazine because they cheered an otherwise drab workplace:

> 'These duller garments [i.e. trousers] are then adorned by the most vividly patterned smock or overall obtainable. Hats off to the designers who have reproduced our English flower gardens in cotton for the factory glows like a herbaceous border with these brilliant overalls.'

The same article encouraged factory workers to assert their femininity by using make-up and bright accessories, including sparkling brooches pinned to turbans or overalls and the wearing of earrings. However, women who placed more emphasis on appearance than safety were sometimes at risk:

> "They had to be very careful with their shoes as well — they got their heels caught in the duckboards that they stood on."

> "I've seen girls lose their hair in the machines ... some of them would stick [their hats] on the back, you know — they liked to be looking glamorous and different. I've seen a girl lose a great bunch of hair — just pulled it out by the roots."

Women's own clothes were not always suitable for wear near machinery and even those who were sensibly dressed could be in danger. One woman, a hairdresser before conscription into an aircraft factory, recalls a near-miss with a metal rolling machine:

> "I worked in my hairdressing overalls and they were very nice poplin and nicely tailored — they had lovely things on the market before the war. Watching the metal go through, the rough edge caught on my overall and it took me up to this machine — these massive big rollers — and it just ripped everything I'd got on right to my skin and the chap on the machine pulled me away just in time ... no guard on the machine or anything like that."

As in the Land Army, factories provided many women with their first experience of wearing trousers. Some liked them so much they bought slacks for wear after work:

> "We wore dungarees at work so we bought trousers [i.e. to go out in] ... I'd never worn trousers before ... it was unheard of before the war — I don't ever remember seeing any woman in trousers, no."

'Immobile' women, unable to work full time in industry because of family commitments, were sometimes able to do part-time work in their own villages. A documentary film entitled *Taking the Work to the Worker* shows women in the Warwickshire village of Kineton doing assembly work in their local telephone exchange and pub function room. The work, delivered and collected by factories in the Midlands, could be done by women working just a few hours daily. Child care could be shared, and the film shows one small child being 'swapped' as mother and grandmother arrive and depart at the telephone exchange. Such workers were not supplied with protective clothing, and wore their own clothes covered with an apron or pinafore.

Large numbers of women served in the armed forces, either as volunteers or conscripts in the A.T.S. (Auxiliary Territorial Service), W.A.A.F. (Women's Auxiliary Air Force), or W.R.N.S. (Women's

"These duller garments are then adorned by the most vividly patterned smock or overall obtainable."

WHAT THEY DO AND WHAT THEY WEAR...

THE AUXILIARY TERRITORIAL SERVICE

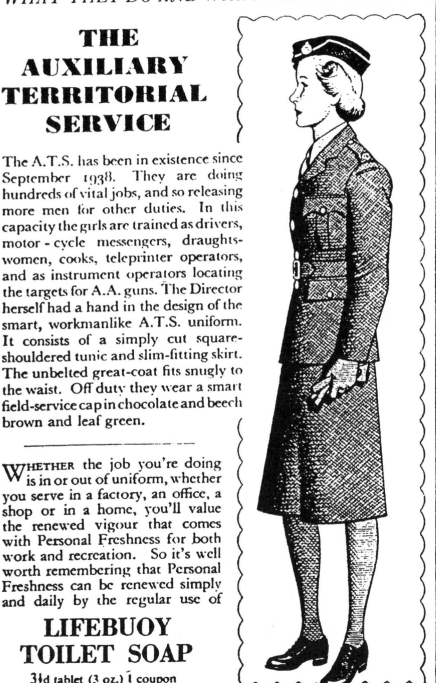

The A.T.S. has been in existence since September 1938. They are doing hundreds of vital jobs, and so releasing more men for other duties. In this capacity the girls are trained as drivers, motor-cycle messengers, draughts-women, cooks, teleprinter operators, and as instrument operators locating the targets for A.A. guns. The Director herself had a hand in the design of the smart, workmanlike A.T.S. uniform. It consists of a simply cut square-shouldered tunic and slim-fitting skirt. The unbelted great-coat fits snugly to the waist. Off duty they wear a smart field-service cap in chocolate and beech brown and leaf green.

WHETHER the job you're doing is in or out of uniform, whether you serve in a factory, an office, a shop or in a home, you'll value the renewed vigour that comes with Personal Freshness for both work and recreation. So it's well worth remembering that Personal Freshness can be renewed simply and daily by the regular use of

LIFEBUOY TOILET SOAP

3½d tablet (3 oz.) 1 coupon

Royal Naval Service). They undertook not only domestic and clerical duties, but work involving technical and mechanical skills and sheer physical strength. Women rebuilt engines and operated barrage balloons, drove and serviced military vehicles, and spent long shifts meticulously plotting the movement of allied and enemy ships and aircraft. Women who had last worn uniform as schoolgirls now found themselves back in it, with overalls and dungarees supplied for the dirty jobs that had to be undertaken.

Some members of the women's forces had little opportunity to wear clothing other than their service uniform. A member of the W.A.A.F. remembers that 'civvies' were worn only on leave: when off duty, they still wore uniform, although for social events like dances they were permitted to remove their jackets (but not their ties). When on leave, many W.A.A.F.s had to make do with pre-war clothes as they were not provided with clothing coupons like their civilian sisters. The W.A.A.F. uniform consisted of skirt, shirt and tie, jacket, greatcoat, shoes, lisle stockings and hat. Skirts had to be seventeen inches above the ground, regardless of height, so that a line of skirts on parade presented a consistent appearance. Underwear was also supplied, and several women rather ruefully remember the knitted interlock knickers, fleecy lined, known as 'passion killers'. There was little that was worn or used that was not supplied by the Air Force, from "bras, blacking and brushes".

The uniform worn by the W.R.N.S. was sometimes claimed to be smarter than that of the other two services. An ex-W.R.N. remembers that her uniform included:

"Two well-made uniforms, one for work and a better one nicknamed a 'tiddly suit', which we promptly had dry cleaned to remove the fluff. Navy blue greatcoat (mine was tailored by Hector Powe!), blue gabardine mac, 2 pairs shoes, 3 white shirts, 3 pairs navy 'directoire' style knickers nicknamed 'Black-outs', and stockings … in the job I did, I was allowed to purchase navy blue skirts, oilskin and 'bell bottoms'. Eight of us shared two duffle coats, all strictly for work."

Fine stockings were for 'going ashore', and this woman, stationed in Scotland, remembers sending home to Leamington for black hosiery:

"The hosiery buyer of the store I had worked at was marvellous, and possibly not so many black stockings were in demand down here … the tailors called these 'tart socks'."

W.R.N.S., unlike women in the W.A.A.F. obtained coupons 'from Admin. P.O.' to purchase items such as stockings.

Members of the A.T.S. were also provided with two uniforms — one for work and the other for 'walking out'. It consisted of skirt and tunic, worn over shirts that had separate collars, with brown shoes, stockings and cap. Underwear was 'issue' and one woman remembers being supplied with two pairs of knickers and vests in cream wool, two pairs of khaki knickers, two bras and two pairs of pyjamas. The 'short sleeve order' permitted women to remove jackets and pull up sleeves in hot weather, but the sleeves were to be *folded* (not rolled) exactly two inches above the elbow — no more, no less. If kit was damaged, lost or stolen, it was replaced — the cost being taken from the woman's wages.

Hair had to be off the collar, although whether all members of the A.T.S. kept it at the regulation two inches above is doubtful. Long hair had to be put up:

"I wore my hair long and rolled it round a piece of tape just to sit nicely around my cap with my hair off my shoulders as we all had to do."

Those entering the forces early in the war spent the subsequent five or six years being told what to wear and how to wear it. Discipline regarding clothes, as with all other facets of service life, was stern and uncompromising, yet many women have no regrets about spending long years in khaki or navy blue. The services provided opportunities for travel, comradeship and responsibility that some women would never have experienced in civilian life:

"As a service woman I enjoyed it very much – although there was discipline, there was comradeship and a feeling of helping one another."

Women who were not in the forces, and therefore not obliged to wear uniform, sometimes adopted a military style of dress:

"During the war many of us who were not in the services liked to dress in a 'military' style so I, for one, wore a dark blue coat with epaulettes and breast pockets .. as I never wore a hat, it was obvious that I wasn't in uniform."

Certain civilian jobs, such as nursing and domestic service, had required women to wear some kind of uniform before 1939. The outbreak of war, however, brought many more into occupations that demanded prescribed clothing – whether as paid employees such as railway guards, or as members of voluntary organizations such as the Women's Voluntary Service. Many women worked in a voluntary capacity, in some cases in addition to their regular employment, and if they did not wear uniform as a paid worker they often did as a volunteer:

A member of the W.A.A.F., or Women's Auxiliary Air Force.

"I qualified as an Air Raid Warden with my father in Moseley, Birmingham, six weeks before the war. During this time they gave us this uniform and our respirators and you had to check people's lighting and go and advise them about the black-out and all that kind of thing. There were A.R.P. posts throughout and we were trained as to where we had to report should there be an emergency ... when the war broke out ... I put on my tin hat and respirator, walked across with Daddy to the A.R.P. centre to man the phone and we all expected to be blown to smithereens in no time, but of course nothing happened for months."

As an air-raid warden, this woman remembers being issued with "... one whistle, one tin hat and gas mask, plus identity card and silver badge which is silver marked."
The uniform itself consisted of:

"... a navy blue corduroy battledress – like Churchill wore – a blouson battledress with pockets, and thick socks and flat shoes; a scarf round my head to take the weight of the helmet ... we also had a navy blue gabardine kind of overall coat with A.R.P. in red on it ... I used to like to feel I felt smart."

The navy A.R.P. boilersuit was her first introduction to 'real' trousers:

"I had had some beach pyjamas – they were quite famous things – wide-legged things, silky, halter neck and backless, but I hadn't actually worn trousers as such, no I hadn't, ever."

Like so many others, she recognized the practicality of trousers both for A.R.P. work and for leaping into when the sirens sounded at night:

"We used to have some cold winters then and it was far easier to get out of bed because I used to stack them [i.e. clothes] in order of putting on when the sirens were going – so socks/stockings first, pants, bra, something warm – trousers – they were much quicker than skirts and all that – no, I didn't mind at all."

Also waiting by the bedside would be gas mask, whistle and hat – always to be taken in an emergency, whatever else was left behind:

"The first thing you put on was your respirator slung over your shoulder and your whistle – the two things you went with and your tin hat, of course – even if you'd got no clothes on!"

In the early 1940s a long hairstyle, drooping seductively over one eye before falling to the shoulders, was popularized by the actress Veronica Lake in the film *I Wanted Wings*. The nature of their war work meant that for many women long hair was impractical, and although the film star was subsequently much photographed with her hair up, the style persisted. While long-haired women in the forces rolled their hair up under their service hats, those in industry wore turbans and snoods to keep long hair safely out of the way. The snood was a net, worn alone or with a hat, that contained the hair at the back of the head. It had been very fashionable in the mid-nineteenth century and was reintroduced by the designer Schiaparelli in 1935. However, it really only came into popular use with the advent of the war, as a means of restraining hair and keeping it tidy. In some factories snoods were supplied, along with other protective clothing –

"All the women and girls had to wear overalls, and matching blue hats with snoods at the back to hold the hair up out of the way" –

and in others women supplied their own:

"Those with long hair wore snoods – a wide-gauge cotton net, all colours – to keep hair tidy."

Many photographs of women at work during the war show them in turbans – scarves bound round the head and tied at the top with the ends tucked neatly away:

"People in the factories used to wear scarves tucked up round their hair like turbans ... I couldn't bear them myself ... I didn't wear one."

Others who 'couldn't bear them' were sometimes involved in appalling accidents as their loose hair became trapped in overhead machinery:

"We had one or two scalpings –they'd have their head down with this vertical drill and their hair would get caught in it."

Many women, even if not compelled to, took to wearing turbans because they were practical, and this applied to those on the land as well as in industry:

"The headscarf seemed to make its debut, or come into its own at this time, and were well used by land girls, as worn turban-wise they protected the hair from dust, spray, chaff and cavings."
[The waste material thrown out by the threshing machines was known as chaff and cavings.]

Some land girls, unwilling to spend coupons on headscarves for work, discovered alternative turbans that were cheap and coupon-free. Several remember buying surgical slings from Boots the Chemist; at around 6d. each they were very inexpensive and two slings — one covering the front of the hair and tied at the back, and the other covering the back and tied at the front — adequately concealed the hair. The same women also remember buying goggles from the Army and Navy Stores to protect the eyes during threshing.

The popularity of scarves may also have been due to the fact that they concealed hair that had travelled from pillow to works bus without coming into contact with a hair brush:

"I think it was during the war that women started wearing headsquares as turbans. Often one could see that under the turban the girls wore curlers in their hair."

In most cases this was not slovenliness. Women rising early and spending long hours on a factory shift did not always have much time to devote to their appearance, particularly when this involved the removal of large numbers of hair curlers:

"I can well remember running down the lane to catch the 6.20 a.m. train, munching a dried egg sandwich, with my hair in curlers but tucked under the triangular scarf — 'turban' — which was quite the vogue then."

"The war years were the start of women wearing headscarves (tied under the chin or as a 'turban') and underneath the women wore their curlers — I can remember having 100 pipe cleaners in my hair, then taking them out one by one and curling the curl around my fingers. I was *very* proud of my curls!"

"We didn't put scarves on like they do now — now they put them on and tie them under the chin — but we used to put them on like turbans. Yes, we used to wear them all the time because in the war we used to have to go to work at 8 o'clock in the morning and sometimes we didn't finish till 8 at night — if there was any special work on we used to have to stay till a particular batch had gone through — so you didn't always have time to play around with your hair."

The nature of their war work not only affected how women dressed, it also had some impact on their physical welfare and appearance. Land girls were particularly susceptible as they laboured through the seasons, spending much of the winter doing rough work in raw weather:

"We did some really hard jobs, especially when we had to go out in the frosty morning and cut off the sprouts — can you imagine it? — growing in a frosty field and they were as hard as iron, and you had these — like machetes almost — and you chopped off these sprouts ... growing in a field that was hard as iron — you still had to do the work so that your hands — yes, they did suffer."

Besides harsh weather, the nature of some of the work itself left land girls looking 'a sorry picture'.

"When I looked in the mirror I had a shock for I presented a sorry picture. Dirt was in the corners of my eyes, up my nostrils and on my lips. There were clean streaks where the sweat had run

Woman Air Raid Warden in uniform.

down my face and I seemed to have lost my pageboy bob. I was a brunette, but thistledown clinging to my hair made me look prematurely grey."

This was the spectacle presented to one land girl when she glanced at her reflection after threshing. She recalls that the *Land Girl* magazine was as original in its medical recommendations as it was in its suggestions for moleskin slippers:

"Aching backs, blisters, and the problem of protecting the eyes when threshing all received their due share of attention in the pages of the *Land Girl*. As a cure for chilblains, a mixture of grated carrots and lard, warmed in the oven and allowed to set, was advised. A salve used for cows udders was recommended for keeping the hands soft. A rotten tomato apparently worked wonders for removing tomato stains from the hands."

"We did some really hard jobs, especially when we had to go out in the frosty morning and cut off the sprouts."

Those working on fruit farms discovered that chemical sprays could have an unexpected effect on hair colour:

"We used to wear these headscarves — turbans, we called them. Everything (i.e. hair) had to be covered. Well, some used to have a little bit out — some girls used to do spraying, you know, the fruit trees — and this spray used to turn their hair really blond ... oh, it was horrible stuff, that was."

While women in industry were not at the mercy of wind and weather and the discomfort of uncongenial tasks such as threshing, their long shifts in the 'shops' under artificial lights could leave them weary, and low in spirit. Factory noise and smells — particularly the stench of 'suds' — were not easy to get used to:

"Suds ... was a liquid that used to run on the drills for certain metals to stop it getting hot — to keep it cool — and the smell of that was dreadful. My mother used to say, 'Don't come in here with that coat on' — I used to have to take all the outside clothes off ... it was horrible. It was like living over a fish and chip shop only a different smell!"

HOUSEWIFE 1944

The Hand that held the Hoover works the Lathe!

With no glamour of uniform, with all the burdens and responsibilities of running a home, thousands of housewives in 1944 are war-workers too. They are doing a double job. They get no medals for it. But if ever women deserved especial honour, these do. So to all war-workers who also tackle shopping queues, cooking, cleaning, mending and the hundred and one other household jobs

Salute! FROM HOOVER

Hoover users know best what improvements they would like in the post-war Hoover. Suggestions are welcome.

BY APPOINTMENT TO H.M. KING GEORGE VI AND H.M. QUEEN MARY
HOOVER LIMITED PERIVALE, GREENFORD, MIDDLESEX

Those in other occupations sometimes considered that factory girls did very well for themselves. Wages were often good — "At one time we were getting £5 a week and we thought that was great after 7/6d." — and canteens provided filling, but cheap, meals. But the long hours meant there was little opportunity for married women to shop for food, and on returning home at the end of a long working day (or night) there were house and children to attend to. Letters to women's magazines asked for advice on treating varicose veins and shadows under the eyes — "I am barely seventeen, yet friends keep saying how tired I look. I have dark shadows under my eyes, too" — along with other complaints that developed as a result of overwork.

Women on night shifts sometimes found it difficult to sleep during the day, when noises from the neighbourhood made undisturbed rest impossible:

"You had to be in the factory by 7.00 p.m., came off at 7.00 a.m. the next morning and home by 7.30 a.m. — breakfast, to bed ... it was very difficult [to sleep] because the neighbours didn't have washing machines in those days — they had the old tub and dolly and on Monday mornings, 'Bang, bang, bang', with the tub and dolly, banging away, and mother said, 'Sleep in our room at the front', so I slept in there, and even then I couldn't sleep for the traffic — we used to get a lot of Army lorries."

The same woman remembers going to the cinema every Wednesday evening when on day shift, but "... sometimes I'd just fall asleep in the pictures."

Even voluntary workers could find their appearance dramatically, if temporarily, altered. One air-raid warden who had worked in the elegant environment of the 'gown trade' remembers being showered with the contents of an allotment during one of her evening patrols:

"One night we were walking up our territory and we were just by a row of trees at the top of the road and there were houses this side and allotments and I suddenly sensed a shooshing noise and I shouted to Daddy and I screamed my head off and they trained you to fall on the floor and arch your back and scream so that the air didn't burst your ear drums ... I fell in that position, Daddy fell on top of me. I screamed my head off — there were five bombs — we were absolutely covered with soil, vegetables — you name it ... when it stopped, I stood up full of great composure and I said, 'Keep calm, everybody, keep calm', and one man said, 'Keep calm be buggered — where's my bloody roof gone?'"

4 Weddings

Before 1939 most brides-to-be anticipated a traditional wedding. This would include a church ceremony in white dress, with accompanying bridesmaids and guests, and a reception to follow – either a lavish wedding breakfast, or a 'bit of a do', according to taste and circumstance. The war disrupted thousands of wedding plans. Couples continued to marry, but often not in the style or manner they had once envisaged.

With many fiancés away from home serving in the forces, it was difficult to plan a wedding at all. Some couples decided to postpone the ceremony and wait in hope of happier times. Others decided to marry anyway, even though this often meant a hasty wedding and subsequent long separation as the bridegroom returned to the Front. Some women found themselves with as little as forty-eight hours in which to prepare: a telegram might arrive from a fiancé saying he would be home on leave in two days, and could the wedding be rushed forward. The bride would dash off to clergyman or registrar, obtain a licence (costing £2.14s.7d. in 1945) and endeavour to make what arrangements she could in the short time available. In such circumstances it was sometimes possible to borrow a dress, but many brides went to the altar in the smartest suit or prettiest day dress they could find, trimmed with a little posy of flowers and topped by an elaborate hat. If, in the forty-eight hours between telegram and ceremony, the bride had any time to spare she might even make a hat herself. Magazine articles provided details for just such hasty constructions: according to one, four bunches of feather flowers stitched to a small circle of buckram could be pinned to the hair, swathed with a length of veil tied at the back in a bow.

One woman remembers a fellow land girl being married from their Land Army hostel. The wedding had been arranged rapidly, and the bride had nothing suitable to wear: the other land girls rallied round and between them furnished the entire wedding outfit, including handbag. Another woman remembers getting married in Birmingham, by special licence, in an outfit stored in the air-raid shelter for safe keeping.

"I was married in August 1941 just a few weeks after clothes rationing started and bought my dress before then. It was moss green crêpe, with hat to match. It cost 12/11d. and the dress was £3.10.0d. Shoes in the same shade of moss green suede with lilac kid wedge heels. They were 12/11d. also. I made the bag with mauve felt and cut out flowers to decorate [it] … My wages were £2.0.0. per week so the outfit was very expensive at the time. I kept the outfit in the air-raid shelter … and afterwards returned it to the shelter for safe keeping."

After travelling into central Birmingham,

"I went to New Street station and changed into my clothes – into the cloakroom at New Street

Many women married in clothes that would be useful after their wedding.

station and changed into my wedding clothes ... we went to the Registry Office and the girl that had taken my job was in the office just round the corner and I asked her to come and be a witness, and my sister-in-law – she worked in the town – I asked her..."

The speed with which some wartime weddings had to be arranged was not the only reason for brides abandoning long white gowns in favour of day dress. After clothes rationing was introduced in 1941, many women were unable or unwilling to spend coupons on a garment that would be worn only once:

"Many girls getting married decided to forgo a traditional white wedding dress, and instead used their precious clothing coupons on an outfit which would be useful after the wedding."

Even if you had enough coupons for a dress, or the fabric to make one, there was no guarantee that you would find what you liked, or the necessary accessories to complete the outfit:

"... it was difficult to get a veil – it was like everything else, they had quarters in – quarter dozens in – and you had your name on a list and I was fortunate to get a veil – a plain veil – and that went to a lot of weddings after mine. Nearly all my friends borrowed the veil."

Wedding rings, essential for propriety if not legality, could also be difficult to obtain – "In early 1944 it was difficult to find a wedding ring" – and after the war ended, supplies did not improve immediately. One woman, marrying after 1945, remembers being unable to obtain a twenty-two carat ring and having to settle for one of nine carat gold.

It was not surprising that, defeated by circumstances, many women settled for a modest wedding in ordinary clothes. One remembers wearing a green wool dress and matching turban, and another that both she and her bridesmaids wore suits. This woman was also married in green:

"1941 – married, wore sage green dress, brown felt hat with a tiny veil over eyes and brown suede court shoes."

While some women did not mind losing their chance of a white wedding –

"It didn't worry me in the least – no, it wasn't a disappointment, I didn't worry about it" –

others deeply regretted it. One woman remembers feeling 'bitterly disappointed' at having to marry in a suit – a disappointment partly alleviated, years later, when she was able to provide a traditional wedding for her daughter.

Some wartime brides were married in white, in spite of difficulties in obtaining fabric. For those marrying before the onset of rationing it was possible to exercise quite a wide choice:

"My wedding dress was of lace and cost just under £4 and I was lucky to have bought it some weeks prior to the wedding day, before coupons were needed."

"There was a nice selection around – I bought mine down in High Wycombe. I didn't buy it locally because a month before I got married my sister got married and she had by that time got all her clothes and I wanted something entirely different and out of the area – so we used to go visiting H___'s [her fiancé] sister who lived at High Wycombe ... I paid eight guineas for my dress ... not necessarily dear – sort of middle of the road."

This woman had six bridesmaids, and a reception for friends and relatives which ended with comic photographs being taken in the garden amongst the cabbages.

After clothes rationing, the choice for white wedding clothes became much more limited. Some women sought out unrationed fabric, and made up dresses from material that had been intended to serve as lace or net curtains:

"When in 1943 I told my mother that I would be getting married she decided that I should have a white wedding. Most people had given up that thought by then, for shops were getting very bare. My mother tracked down some lace or net which wasn't on coupons — white for me and pink for bridesmaids. These were made into dresses which had slips underneath. I believe I wore a white silk nightie under mine ... my mother even scrounged or saved enough supplies to make a three-tier cake and do all the food."

Wedding reception near Coventry. The real bride, with bouquet, is sixth from the left.

Others were able to beg coupons from family and friends in order to buy not only their own dress but those of the bridesmaids too:

"We were most enthusiastic in begging coupons from friends and relations and some lovely wedding dresses were made, to be later passed round and altered and used several times."

"We married on January 29th 1944 at St Mary's Church, Warwick and afterwards held the reception at the Court House – my future father-in-law did not go out so you see I was able to use his clothing coupons, because we had to give coupons up for two bridesmaids dresses and shoes as well … I went to Birmingham for my ivory-coloured wedding dress, cost £18. I remember going into a cubicle to try it on and then was told to walk out into the large shopping area with the large mirrors. It was beautiful and I felt like a queen and someone said, 'Look', and when I turned all the area outside the shop people were waving and wishing me luck … I can remember we had to pay ten shillings to use the piano in the ballroom to have a sing song. We had a two-tiered wedding cake, made by a baker, but I'm afraid we had to pay black market prices for some of the food."

"We married on January 29th 1944 at St Mary's Church, Warwick…"

White wedding dresses could also be borrowed or hired, and sometimes one dress was used many times as it passed between different members of a family and their friends:

"My dress had belonged to my step-sister, she was married just before the war. It had been an expensive dress but she was about two sizes bigger than me so had to be altered but still looked a bit shapeless ... the bridesmaid's dresses were satin — one pink and the other lilac — borrowed — the dresses were different styles but at least the head-dresses matched."

"The person I was lodging with — the daughter — she lent me hers but I bought a new veil ... if you'd bought a new one [dress] it would've taken all your coupons and it's only for one day, isn't it?"

"I didn't have a new one — I had my brother's sister-in-law's. She was my build and she'd only worn it the once and she offered it to me and I thought, 'Well, here goes. I shall be able to buy the bridesmaid's material then with the coupons.' I would have preferred a new one, but we'd lived through five years of war and you got used to being without."

Some women needed only to borrow a veil:

"My wedding dress was made out of something called 'Angel Skin' which was really, I suppose, one of the early synthetics. It had a lovely sheen. I borrowed a veil — there was a great line of borrowing and I made a head-dress of white artifical camellia-type flowers."

"My dress had belonged to my step-sister, she was married just before the war."

This particular woman, with access to the London markets, had little difficulty in finding fabric, and the coupons were 'bought' – or purchased from others who had some to spare:

"You knew where your markets were to go and buy material. We had two bridesmaids – the dresses weren't full or lavish, they were simple."

Even women in the services, far from home and family, sometimes managed a white wedding.

"I remember going to a wedding in Cairo and the girl had hired a dress all the way from England – she did look lovely with the foreign scented flowers."

Flowers for the bouquet could be another source of difficulty. Several women, on looking back at their wedding photographs, have commented on how large bouquets of the time were:

"We'd like to point out the bouquets to you – they were so big – lots of ferns. They were so heavy you could hardly hold them – they were on a stick or handle – they went up your arm, sort of thing! Ridiculous really – those little ones they have today are so much nicer and neater, aren't they?"

If fresh flowers could not be obtained, bride and bridesmaids made do with artificial ones:

"There were no fresh flowers but we found some artificial ones – very similar to today's silk flowers."

Another woman remembers that while she had a bridal bouquet from the florist, her bridesmaids were supplied with lilac from the gardens of friends and neighbours:

"My aunt was a florist and she managed, from the shop where she was working, to make it up there – they were red and white carnations. Theirs [bridesmaids] are lilac – various friends and neighbours, I think their trees were stripped and of course it was just about the right time – the lilac was at its very best – it was the dark lilac."

Food for a wedding reception could also prove difficult, as food, like clothes, was rationed. Families who did scrape together enough coupons for a culinary celebration were sometimes forced to compromise – even over the centrepiece, the wedding cake:

"Managed to get together sugar and fruit for the wedding cake but not for icing – the catering firm did a wonderful job, but had to lift off the cardboard 'icing' to cut the cake."

Friends, relatives and neighbours were often called upon to help provide food, or food coupons, for the reception:

"We had friends – people clubbed together and helped each other out – we had a wonderful wedding, weren't short of anything."

Co-operation meant that it was usually possible to concoct a wedding cake, although there were not always enough coupons to buy ingredients for the icing:

"... all the neighbours had put their fat ration and their sugar ration and their bits of currants together and made us a cake, so we did have a cake for our wedding."

It was inevitable that, in the unusual conditions of wartime, weddings, receptions and honeymoons (if you were lucky enough to have one) were marred by incidents both trivial and tragic. One woman remembers that while her own wedding proceeded smoothly,

"that same evening another wedding party was taking place in Birmingham. They were all killed when a bomb dropped on them."

"1940 — married at St John's, Leamington Spa, the same day as a land mine dropped on 'The Globe' public house killing twenty people."

Other difficulties merely caused inconvenience. One couple who travelled to Blackpool for their honeymoon found the beach inaccessible:

"We went to Blackpool for a week but you couldn't get near the sea for barbed wire — all barbed wire around the coast. We couldn't get on the sands."

Another pair, having married at very short notice and been given several days holiday, found themselves outside their first honeymoon hotel minutes after setting foot inside it:

"We went to book into a hotel and of course he said, 'Will you sign the register?' and I went to put 'Ca' instead of 'Ba'. 'Oh no,' he said, 'we don't allow that kind of thing here.' So on my wedding day I was in tears. Anyway, we finally did manage to find somewhere to stay for the rest of the week, and that was that."

Couples booking into hotels and guest houses had to present their food ration books and one woman remembers this was pointed out when she received confirmation of her booking from her chosen hotel.

"I remember going to a wedding in Cairo and the girl had hired a dress all the way from England..."

Another couple, spending their honeymoon with a relative, were asked to bring a sewing machine as the family wished to make some clothes. They travelled not only with the machine, but the bridegroom's mother:

"When we got there (Coventry station) these airforce boys who were in transit somewhere or other were all round the canteen having tea, but of course when they see a wedding car come up – eyes on it, naturally – and they were highly amused to see us getting out and then when the luggage came out the back – the sewing machine came as well as mother.

Oh, they did comment, yes. They said, 'Oh, look – not only mother-in-law but a sewing machine as well!' I suppose we must have struck a funny picture to them."

In spite of the difficulties occasioned by clothes rationing, many women attempted to put together some kind of trousseau in preparation for their wedding. The trousseau did not always include the range and quality of garments that would have been expected before the war, and many of them were of the 'Make-do-and-mend' variety:

"I did make a kind of trousseau out of some kind of purply colour lace, and a chiffon nightie that I made and some ribbon because you couldn't buy anything like that."

Parachutes, which provided numerous women with underclothes and nightdresses, were eagerly sought out for the making of a trousseau, particularly if they were of white or cream silk:

"I even had a parachute when I got married to make undies – white parachute silk. I made French pants and I even tried to make a bra, believe it or not..."

"As I was in the W.R.N.S. I was well supplied with clothing during the war, but as I got married in 1947 I needed more glamorous underwear than service issue. This I made from silk and nylon parachutes, superfluous to requirements. I cannot remember where we bought them, but it was quite legal as far as I remember. It was not an easy task as they consisted of long narrow triangles cut on the cross. The silk was good and lasted me until rationing ended, but the nylon was very thin and clammy."

Women marrying after 1945 looked forward to marriage as a new start in a post-war world, although austerity continued well beyond the war's end:

"War was over and you felt that real austerity should be behind you so then you started wanting more than one slip – one in the wash and one on – and as marriage is supposed to be a new start I think you thought that way, and I had this slip and pants from parachute silk and they were all embroidered with a different motif."

Other women saved nylons that they had received as gifts, and kept them in the bottom drawer for their wedding day:

"My brother was in the navy and he was down in Durban and he brought me back some nylons and that was in 1946 and I wasn't married till 1947, and the tips we were given, as you would say, we were told to put them in screw top jars and that's what I did – and kept it in the bottom of my drawer."

Few women marrying during the war, or for several years after its end, were able to wear the outfit of their choice. This is not generally remembered with disappointment — on the contrary, weddings are described with pride as a celebration for which friends and family pooled resources to provide all the essentials, from dress and veil to currants for the cake.

Friends and neighbours provided lilac for these bouquets.

"... very often we went out in uniform."

5 Dressing-up

While weddings were events for which everyone tried to dress up, other opportunities for 'dressiness' were much curtailed by the war. Lavish or frivolous dressing was no longer possible or appropriate for most occasions, and for some women the occasions themselves dwindled along with their wardrobes. Factory workers on long shifts, including nights, did not always have the time or the energy to go 'gallivanting':

"We didn't have a lot of time to go gallivanting because you worked on a rota — there was no Saturdays and Sundays off."

"Really, people didn't worry so much about clothes — there was nowhere to go — nowhere to wear best clothes."

Those land girls billeted at isolated farmhouses were very much cut off from a regular social life, and unless the nearest town was within cycling distance their chances of evenings out were limited.

Conversely, other young women had increased opportunities for socializing during the war, particularly if they were in an area where troops were stationed. Dances were extremely popular, but women were not always able to dress up for them in the style they would have wished. Women in the forces danced as they worked — in uniform, although they were permitted to remove their jackets in the dance hall.

Land girls also wore uniform off duty. This was partly to save wear and tear on their civilian clothing —

"In fact we had so few clothes of our own that we seldom went out in 'civvies'. We did wear them occasionally but very often we went out in uniform" —

and partly because uniforms were more practical for cycling to venues. The Land Army provided bicycles for its members, although some women do not remember them with much fondness:

"They were new — they were all new to start with but they weren't very good — they were just thrown together — nothing stylish about them. They had great thick tyres and great thick mudguards."

It was on these unstylish bicycles that some land girls turned up at dances:

"A lot of land girls wore their uniforms when off duty, they were practical for cycling long distances to dances and events of a social nature — transport in the country being very sparse.

Also, the wearing of uniform made it easier to hitch lifts and gain other concessions such as using forces canteens. It also preserved one's civilian clothes."

Occasionally, land girls would dress up for a particular occasion and surprise each other in the process:

"Everyone enjoyed that party. We derived a huge kick from dressing up for it, and the bathrooms smelled like beauty parlours. Most of us lived in slacks in the evenings, and as a visit to the Sergeants' Mess or a dance at The Hut involved a long cycle ride on a cold evening we tended to wear our walking-out uniform of greatcoat, green jersey and best gabardine breeches. Consequently we had never seen each other dressed up and some of the transformations were quite remarkable."

(*Librarian in the Land Army*, Dorothea Abbott)

Women civilians attending dances tended to wear short summer dresses or blouses and skirts:

"We wanted to keep up our appearances because we always wanted to look nice — we used to dress up — but not evening dress, only in the very select places but not in our local hops — just a summer dress, something frilly and flouncy, a skirt and a blouse, but nearly everyone could find something."

Sometimes the same one or two dresses had to be worn Saturday after Saturday, as rationing made 'frivolous purchases' out of the question:

"During the war the only social occasions were the dances held in the local halls. The girls from the 'respectable' and well-known families in the town were issued with passes to these dances. My first dance frock was made from a white cotton material with a green leaf motif. It was bought from a stall on the local market and I ran it up on my mother's sewing machine. My second dance frock was of a multi-coloured flowered patterned material. I bought it second hand from a local Church bazaar stall. With the issue of clothing coupons any further frivolous purchases were impossible and these two dresses together with the shoes were worn for the rest of the war years."

Women attending grander ·functions, in the 'select places', also modified their dress. While continuing to be smart, they abandoned fussy and elaborate long dresses in favour of simpler evening wear. If an evening dress was made it had to be cunningly contrived for wear on many occasions:

"I had a blue dress ... which was a kind of moiré taffeta — in a deep blue, and it was made in three parts — the skirt on the band and a shirred top with straps which literally hooked onto the skirt underneath, and a little bolero. That came out one year and then the next year I had a silver lamé-type bodice which hooked on — you always had to think — two or three..."

There was a lot of help and co-operation between women, both in the home and in the workplace. If someone was going to a particular event then friends and colleagues would lend garments and accessories, and perhaps provide help with hair or nails:

"In the factory the girls would help each other, do things for each other — do their hair, make them up and things like that."

"I think people seemed to do a lot for each other, because someone in the office was a manicurist before she came in and she used to do our nails at lunch time — a lot of sharing — if someone was going somewhere special your blouse would go with her skirt — yes, there was a lot of that."

For some women dressing up involved applying make-up as well as stepping into a smart dress, but as the war progressed buying cosmetics became more difficult. Certain toiletries disappeared altogether, while others were in short supply. Perfume was extremely hard to come by:

"It was wonderful to get a drop of perfume — 'Evening in Paris' and 'Californian Poppy' were the favourite."

BOURJOIS
and the Factory Front

MEN'S LIVES depend on the precision of women's work. Their hours are long. Their leisure brief. But you'd never think so to look at them. Give them a moment at the end of a shift, alone with mirror and beauty box and they'll radiate all the freshness and sparkle they had eight hours before. Bourjois realise how much beauty aids mean to women at war. That's why everything possible is being done to see that the limited supplies of their 'Evening in Paris' Beauty Preparations are fairly distributed. That's why they ask you to use them sparingly. Bourjois regret that there is no more 'Evening in Paris' Perfume until after the war, but you can still enjoy the exquisite thrill' of it in their other beauty aids.

BOURJOIS'
'Evening in Paris'

SERVES THE WOMEN WHO SERVE

'Evening in Paris' Powder · Cream · Lipstick
Rouge · Soap · Hair Preparations

'Evening in Paris' went out of production for the duration, but advertisements reassured women that the fragrance was still available in some of the manufacturer's other products.

Some manufacturers continued to advertise their product long after it had become a 'fragrant memory'. Atkinsons kept their Eau de Cologne in the public eye with advertisements offering reassurance on the state of Tunisian orange groves: they ceased production in 1940, but advertisements still appeared five years later, in 1945.

The manufacture of well-known brands of cosmetics was reduced by government order to one quarter of normal output and factory space was given over to the assembly of machine parts and other items essential to the war effort. Advertisements explained to would-be customers why certain products were scarce, and exhorted customers not to settle for brands of inferior quality. A hairdresser who had always sold cosmetics to her customers remembers that supplies were difficult to obtain from the wholesaler:

"I used to sell a small amount of cosmetics but everything was rationed so you'd get a quarter of cream one week and a quarter of lipsticks (a quarter of a dozen I'm talking about) another."

Women kept their eyes open and bought cream or lipstick when they saw it:

"You bought it when you could, if you ever saw it – whether it was your colour or not – if it was a lipstick or something like that you bought it … things used to go like wildfire."

Cosmetics were important morale boosters – "… my lipstick and my engagement ring were two protections against Hitler. I'd never go out without those" – and the vivid brightness of nail polish and lipstick may have compensated for clothes that lost colour through being overworn and overwashed:

"There used to be some lipstick called 'Tangee' and it was orange in the stick and it used to come out a very dark red and it tasted horrible. It was one hundred per cent indelible and you could not get it off, which was good, but it dried your lips up … it wasn't very readily available in any case during the war."

Those working in large cities seem to have had rather less trouble in buying face-creams and make-up, although supplies could not always be guaranteed:

"We used to go to Leadenhall Market and you could always buy Nivea cream. You could always buy there. When I worked in Berkeley Square you were near Soho … I don't say you could always go every Friday but you'd go one week and find they'd got this, another week you'd find they'd got that and I don't remember things being extortionately priced."

When talking about the purchase of cosmetics, women sometimes use the phrase 'under the counter'. By this they mean that shopkeepers did not always display goods openly, but kept some back for sale to regular and favoured customers.

"You'd have to know someone who knew someone that had got it – so much of this stuff never came over the counter – it was always a question of – 'Oh, they've got something in up the road' and you went … you'd ask (in the shop) and I think it was a question of whether your face fitted or not, really – I think this applied with food as well."

Many women had only been used to unscented soaps such as carbolic before the war –

"Before the war we never used to have scented soap – we used to have washing soap – we used to get washed and bathed with washing soap."

"Just the basic carbolic and that kind of thing" –

but even these unglamorous commodities were 'on coupons' for much of the decade. One woman, a nurse, remembers being very pleased to receive gifts of soap from patients:

"Soap, I remember, was difficult – I remember we used to have presents from some of the patients and we were very grateful."

Manufacturers tailored their advertisements to suit the changing times, presenting soap as an alternative to expensive beauty treatments, or a fighter of infections lurking on the hands of factory workers. Lux claimed that its soap went twice as far as rival products because its lather was richer, and included tips for making soap last longer in its advertisements.

"If you'd got anything like Lux you really looked after it, you know … care for it and dry it out so's it lasted and if you did buy soap you'd keep it in an airing cupboard until it got very dry, very hard and then it used to last twice as long … that's what they did and if you got a big stock of soap it was good because it used to get very hard and last…"

Although cosmetics were often in short supply, it was still possible to make regular visits to the hairdresser.

Some of the women decided to adopt a short hairstyle because it was practical – "I kept the short hair style adopted during the war for convenience" – and some hairdressers offered the 'Liberty cut':

"… they used to do – what did they call it? – the 'Liberty cut' – and that was almost like a man's haircut – just cut back like that so that it was very easy to look after."

Not all women wished to be shorn. Many continued to wear their hair long in a variety of styles, which they either dressed themselves or had set and permed into waves at the hairdressers. Hairdressing materials were not as hard to come by as cosmetics:

"Hairdressing materials – that wasn't too bad – it was something to boost the morale and that was something that was kept going – it was cosmetics and things that were scarce."

"You could have a hair-do – oh yes, that was about the one thing you could do."

For women unable to be lavish in other areas of their appearance, a visit to the hairdresser perhaps did give a boost to morale, and even very young women went as often as once a week.

"I used to have my hair done every Saturday afternoon."

"The perms weren't like they are today, they were these things strung up to the ceiling on wires, you know, with hot things coming down and all round – awful. There was no difficulty getting in and it wasn't very expensive."

One woman, attached to a perming machine in the middle of an air raid, refused to be unstrung for fear of ruining her perm and remained in the salon while the staff dived for shelter:

"I had a perm during the war which was the most frightening experience ... it was called a Eugene perm and they rolled your hair into a huge great machine which was like a circle with all these wires coming down and you were virtually strung up to this big machine, you see, and the heat would penetrate ... I'd just got strung up to this thing and the air raid warning went, so the little junior who was helping and the assistant suddenly went quite white and said, 'Oh, we've got to turn the heat off because of fire, we've got to go into the shelter.' I thought, 'Well, the chances of me being bombed are very much less than of my hair being ruined', so I said, 'Well, if I take full responsibility will you leave my hair on the machine, but will you be sure to come up so that it doesn't frizz-out?' And they did. I had to sign a form to say it was my responsibility ... I was only scared twice during the war and that was one of them. Didn't feel very nice being strung up to that thing ... that was the last perm of that calibre that I ever had!"

Factories also provided the opportunity for hair-do's. Sometimes this was 'unofficial', as ex-hairdressers performed on their fellow workers at lunch breaks:

"I used to do a bit in the factory in my lunch hour, as well — no dryers of course, just set it and leave it with all the pins in — take pot luck."

Some factories ran hairdressing clubs where perms were cheap, but workers had no control over when they were likely to take place:

"In the factories they used to run these clubs where you paid one shilling a week and you drew out a number and whatever number came out that was your week to go and have your hair done — that's true, so I had many perms like that which I wouldn't have been able to have afforded..."

Other women made do at home, using whatever shampoos and preparations that came to hand, before fashioning their hair into the large sausage curls or 'Victory Roll' styles that became so popular:

"My mother was always for washing our hair at home. I used to like to go to the hairdressers but she used to use good old fashioned soap ... or Sunlight washing soap."

"We used to wear our hair in a sausage roll around our heads, and when it got too heavy for this style we would wear a snood at the back of our heads, which was a coarse net. Shampoos and soap became scarce and I used to wash mine in Green's soft soap and rinse it with lemon balm steeped in warm water, which gave the hair a lovely shine and a pleasant smell."

When women stepped out before the war, their neatly coiffured heads usually rested beneath a hat of some description. This was true whether they were attending a wedding or simply popping out for a pound of sausages, and of young women as well as old.

"We all had to go and register between a certain age — now this was registering for work ... and I remember I had a big hat on with a very wide brim — lots of net around it — and the girls behind the counter were more enthralled with the hat."

A Film-Star Complexion
can still be yours—

For you can make Lux Toilet Soap last twice as long

OF course you want your complexion to be cared for with the soap-and-water beauty treatment of the film stars. What girl doesn't ? But it's because so many of you are asking for Lux Toilet Soap, that it's often hard to get it in the shops.

Still there's no need to worry. Luckily for us all, Lux Toilet Soap can be made to go twice as far !

You see, the lather made by Lux Toilet Soap is more abundant than the lather made by ordinary soaps. So, with one simple twist of the tablet you get enough lather, even in hard water, to soap your hands and arms. In soft water, you'll get enough for your face and neck as well.

What's more, Lux Toilet Soap lather is *active*. It lasts longer — doesn't dry up and disappear.

And here's a point to remember. To make soap last longer keep it as dry as you can. Never allow it to float about in the bath or basin, or in a watery dish. And when you're near the end of a tablet, stick the remaining piece to the new tablet.

Lux Toilet Soap is now sold in the new 3½d. tablet (Purchase Tax included).

LUX TOILET SOAP
The Beauty Soap of the Film Stars

TL 1255-396   A *LEVER* PRODUCT

Hats, unlike shoes and clothes, did not require coupons and were therefore available to anyone with the money to buy them. They offered one outlet for extravagance, and many plain Utility suits were topped by large and elaborate headwear. But although hats were not officially rationed, they became scarcer as materials and labour were directed to the military rather than the civilian market. In April 1942 *Housewife* magazine wrote:

"If you arrive at your favourite hat shop and see 'No fur felt' written upon the door don't be surprised. Fur felt is getting scarce. Straw is going – or gone – with the wind. Hats are not rationed – and not likely to be – but they go up and up in price."

Some milliners created new hats from men's disused silk toppers, or remodelled customer's old ones. If this was too costly, women could always attempt to make a hat themselves and magazines told them how to do it. According to one article, all that was needed was a hood, pudding basin, millinery wire and an odd piece of fabric, but if transforming such materials into something wearable was too daunting, then trimming an old hat might do instead. This involved taking a very plain, basic model and adding ribbon, bows, feathers, lace, flowers or anything else that might bring variety.

In 1942 the President of the Board of Trade, recognizing that hats were becoming scarcer, wrote to the Archbishop of Canterbury asking him to announce that it was not improper for women to come hatless to Church.

"We didn't wear them. That was when we were allowed to stop wearing them in Church ... that was when those blinkin' headscarves came into fashion."

Those 'blinkin' headscarves' replaced hats on the heads of many of Britain's women. They were much more practical for the active lives that women had to lead, and were adopted by all classes.

"Hats became rather scarce, but as most of us had to ride bicycles we wore headscarves. It was amazing how people would adapt them into quite nice headgear by pleating and folding them to look like hats."

Scarves sold in shops were sometimes quite striking in colour and design, as were those made at home from less orthodox fabrics:

"We went into scarves. You see life became much more informal and you wore a scarf tied under and I had scarves which were old parachute maps – nylon printed parachute maps. You could buy them, I don't know where, and they were printed for use in aircraft to locate where they were and you would get them of all different areas of the world ... they were fashionable – you just hemmed round them and it was a headscarf or a neckscarf."

The wearing of turbans and snoods was not limited to the workplace – "... going out in the evening we used to wear a lot of snoods ... very fashionable" – although in some cases the effect must have been a little startling:

"Turbans, pixi-hoods and snoods which fitted closely round the head and could be quickly pulled on on the way to the air raid shelter at the bottom of the garden in the middle of the night ... I once had a green velvet turban-shaped hat with two 'rabbit's ears' sticking up in the centre, inspired by the design of a barrage balloon."

Women do not seem to think that wearing little but uniform or having fewer opportunities for dressing-up made them feel unfeminine. Some say they never gave it a thought, having more important things to worry about, and —

"You still liked the boys and you still went out and had boyfriends and so — they accepted that you were in uniform."

GAY LITTLE BOWS

Make Them Of Petersham Ribbon
For Your Felt Hat

It is difficult sometimes to know just how to dress up a plain hat quickly. These natty bows can be made in no time and provide just that perfect "different" look. You can make larger bows from wider ribbon in exactly the same way.

1. First take a piece of ribbon 7 inches long and 1 inch wide for the main part of the bow. Make a pleat lengthwise in the centre of the ribbon and stitch it firmly.

2. Make a similar pleat at each end of the ribbon, fold the ends back towards the centre, and stitch them firmly in the centre of the ribbon, thus making two loops.

3. For the bow ends cut two pieces of ribbon about 2½ inches long and pleat one end of each piece. Stitch one pleated end in the centre of the bow, in front, and slanting upwards. Stitch the other end behind the bow slanting in the opposite direction. Shape the ends neatly.

4. To make the "knot," take a piece of ribbon about 2½ inches long, pleat it lengthwise, sew it over the centre of the bow and stitch it firmly at the back.

5. The Finished Bow. It measures about 3¾ inches long, but smaller or larger bows can be made in exactly the same way. It is sometimes called the "Milliners'" Bow and sometimes the "Butterfly" Bow, and looks as if it is made from one strip of ribbon, although it is actually in four pieces.

Dior's 'New Look', October 1947.

6 After the War: the 'New Look'

The war ended in 1945. Germany surrendered on May 7th and Japan on August 14th, but there was no immediate return to 'normality'. It was some time before servicemen and women were able to come home to friends and family, and civilians were unable to indulge in free spending to restock larders and wardrobes. Austerity persisted long after the war itself had come to an end, and clothes rationing remained in force until the spring of 1949 when controls were removed from a large range of garments, which then became coupon-free. Those with money could buy, but choice for many was still limited by high prices and the fact that only a proportion of fabrics was available for the home market.

During the war itself most women seem to have accepted the restrictions placed upon them without resentment, recognizing that there were more important things to worry about than dress:

"Oh no, that was the *least* important thing of your entire existence. You were just pleased to wake up in the morning ... you never seemed to bother about anything you hadn't got – no, it didn't occur to you."

Some do admit to a sense of frustration, however –

"It was so frustrating, not much fun, living from day to day for six long years, not knowing when or how it would end" –

and this increased when hostilities actually ceased:

"We very much wanted to get back to before. I was in my twenties and was very conscious that we'd had to patch and darn, patch and darn; you wanted to get back into nice clothes."

Some women think that conditions became more austere in the immediate post-war period, and those planning weddings as their fiancés were demobbed had as much trouble buying dress or fabric as wartime brides had done.

Servicewomen who had spent the war in uniform looked forward to a return to civilian dress – "After wearing uniform it was nice to get into civvy clothes" – but the clothing coupons they received on leaving the forces did not allow them to buy many new garments, and after purchasing one or two major items such as a coat or suit they had few coupons left for much else:

"When I left the Land Army I was given a few clothing coupons and I was able to have a new coat. My mother found the material for a new dress. The only dresses for several years were what my mother made for me."

Women who had served in the armed forces received a gratuity as well as clothing coupons, and one remembers spending both on a coat:

"Demobbed late 1945 with £28 and clothing coupons, used both on a Beaver lamb coat — real — wore it that winter, husband returned early 1946, and by that winter I was pregnant and still wearing the coat, looking and feeling like a giant panda!"

Another woman also spent cash and coupons on a Beaver lamb coat, but had enough money left over for a bicycle as well!

The first major challenge to the severely tailored style of wartime garments was the launching of the 'New Look' by Christian Dior in February 1947. Some women still remember it with great enthusiasm, even if they never wore a 'New Look' garment themselves:

"Oh yes, that was magic — absolute pure magic seeing that. I still think that was one of the nicest looks there was ... I never remember having anything in that particular style because it was for little waists and the smallest my waist ever was was twenty-eight..."

Dior's new silhouette had narrow shoulders, a rounded bust (padded if necessary), and a little nipped-in waist with very long, full skirt falling over padded hips. When *Picture Post* reported from Paris on the Autumn Collections of 1947, it described one Dior evening dress as having an eighteen inch waist and fifty yards of material in the skirt. Another designer, Jacques Fath, also showed long skirts but his were so pencil-thin and tight as to impede the progress of the most agile of women. The garments were lavish and ostentatiously feminine, some being meticulously crafted with embroidery and beadwork crowded on to the bodices of evening gowns. They were also expensive. Some women remember seeing versions of the 'New Look' in British shops and feeling that it marked a new beginning:

"We thought that was fantastic — yes, quite fantastic — that little nipped-in waist and little short boleros — oh yes, that was beautiful ... that was when people started getting interested in clothes again ... I think his idea was to make women look like women again rather than just look like sacks of potatoes."

One woman thought the 'New Look' represented —

"... an expression that everything was going to be different and new and more lavish ... the use of yards and yards of material. There was this need to get away from this semi-masculine influence ... although it was very unpopular politically..."

It was certainly controversial. Critics commented that in post-war Europe few women had the money to buy, or leisure to wear, such extravagant garments. They regarded it as a reactionary fashion, which looked back to the days of the leisured woman who had little to do but sit in tight corsets amidst yards of skirts. As such, they claimed, the 'New Look' was totally unsuitable for the times. Feminists deplored it as frivolous and trivial, while in Britain politicians denounced it as wasteful. The Labour M.P. Mrs Mabel Ridealgh attacked the 'New Look' vigorously in the *Daily Herald* of 22nd February 1948. She called it —

"[an] utterly ridiculous, stupidly exaggerated waste of material and manpower, foisted on the average woman to the detriment of other, more normal clothing ... the average housewife won't buy it. She can't afford the coupons, let alone the price."

In Britain, 'New Look' garments required so much material that they could only appear in non-Utility ranges, and production of these was still limited. However, by spring 1948 the fashion had become popular here, and as manufacturers modified the style for general wear, the more extreme versions did not feature in most High Streets. Mrs Ridealgh's 'average woman' may not have bought a 'New Look' coat or dress, but that did not prevent her from enjoying the sight of them in shop windows:

"In '47 the 'New Look' came in and that was very long and everybody went mad on that then — I remember seeing it in Debenham's — well, it was Smith's then — seeing them in the window. The 'New Look'!"

Women who had spent the war in dungarees, military uniform or 'Make-do-and-mend', looked on the new fashion as a tonic, although some concede that it was extreme:

"I remember someone coming into the office wearing it and I thought it was a bit extreme because we'd been used to this very military look really, with the square shoulders … it looked better on taller people."

High Street version of the 'New Look': coat with narrow waist and long, full skirt.

Some were unable to buy –

"I married in September 1947 and managed to 'find' enough coupons for a dress and a suit (I hired my wedding dress) only to have Dior's 'New Look' come immediately afterwards rendering my treasured new clothes hopelessly short!" –

and those who could were restricted, by cost and coupons, to one or two items. Some bought something practical – "My next coat was a 'New Look', very long and very shaped, tweed" – while others splashed out on the thoroughly frivolous:

"It was lovely ... I've still got two dresses. They were so nice – they were mid-calf length or longer and very full skirts and very pretty tops ... In 1947 I went to Cambridge as a staff nurse and this is when I began to get more money and all these lovely things came into the shops – this 'New Look' ... I remember buying a dance frock – it was taffeta in bright violets and rose colour mixture – dark blues – and the skirt was very full with a tie at the back and puff sleeves with little bows on the side ... we used to go to May Balls, the war was finished now, we used to go on the river. It was lovely."

The 'New Look', like most fashions, came and went swiftly. In its extreme form it was unsuitable for women who still queued and worked, but it did instigate a more 'feminine' style and a move away from the severe, square garments of wartime.

By 1949, when most clothes restrictions were lifted, many of the women who had been young, single and working ten years before were now wives and mothers:

"I cannot recall much more of those days – by 1945 I had three children and life seemed one round of washing, daily and by hand, meals and sewing and mending."

Any reviving personal interest in fashion was now curtailed, not by official restriction, but by domestic circumstance as women who had built aircraft and laboured on the land strived to raise their children and furnish their homes.

Few resent their youth being passed in military uniform, grubby overalls or renovated dresses. Fashion, or the absence of it, during the war became for them a triviality – 'just a trifle' – and therefore not a subject worthy of much worry or thought:

"Nothing was important – the only thing that was important was for our fellas to come back safely. That was all that interested us – we were all the same..."